*Easy to prepare . . . Fun to make . . .
Marvelous to eat!*

Is there a better way to describe Mennonite cooking?

Here is your chance to try some *Pfeffernusse* . . . or *Funny Cake Pie* . . . or, if you're not that adventurous, a delicious *Cheese and Noodle Ring* from recipes which have been kitchen-tested by Mennonite families for generations. Try them all—all 200 in this tasty Sampler. You'll love them!

FAVORITE FAMILY RECIPES
from the

MENNONITE COMMUNITY COOKBOOK

MARY EMMA SHOWALTER
Drawings by NAOMI NISSLEY

HERALD PRESS   SCOTTDALE, PENNSYLVANIA

FAVORITE FAMILY RECIPES FROM
THE MENNONITE COMMUNITY COOKBOOK

Paperback edition manufactured by Keats Publishing, Inc.,
for Herald Press

Herald Press edition published April, 1972
          Second Printing, October, 1972

ISBN: 0-8361-1682-8

Printed in the United States of America

CONTENTS

INTRODUCTION

A MONG THE COOKBOOKS ON THE PANTRY SHELF AT home there has always been the little hand-written notebook of recipes. As a child I learned that this blue notebook, which contained a collection of my mother's favorite recipes, was her favorite cookbook.

Not only were all the pages of this notebook filled with recipes, but inserted between the pages were loose sheets of paper on which were written other favorites. These were copied by friends and relatives whom Mother had visited at some time and whose specialty she had admired. The recipes were usually named for the donor and thus the book contained many queer names, such as "Grandmother's Ginger Cakes" and "Aunt Emma's Fat Cakes."

As a child I occasionally visited my grandmother and an aunt in an adjoining county. They always had such delicious things to eat, and I noticed that they too frequently referred to quaint little hand-written notebooks similar to my mother's.

As a student in high school I took home economics and was delighted to learn of many new and beautifully illustrated cookbooks. The time had come when I felt I had outgrown that old-time notebook; so I pushed it aside while I tried out new recipes.

Then came college days and frequent visits to my roommate's home in Lancaster County, Pennsylvania. In the heart of that region, where Pennsylvania Dutch cookery abounds, I suddenly became aware of the fact that handwritten notebooks of recipes were still in use.

My first position after finishing college took me throughout the United States. En route I chanced to visit numerous Mennonite communities. I soon began to observe that wherever I went, to California or Colorado, to Iowa or Ohio, our cooking was much the same. Some of the recipes that my mother had recorded in her little book were being used even in the Far West.

Since a cookbook of the favorite recipes of Mennonite families had never been published, I now began to sense that the handwritten recipe books were responsible. I asked to see them wherever I went and was astonished to learn how many of them had been destroyed in recent years. The daughters of today were guilty of pushing them aside in favor of the new, just as I had done one day. It is true that many of our mothers were still using the old favorite recipes, but were doing so by memory. When I found them, the little notebooks were usually at the bottom of a stack of modern cookbooks and were kept only for memory's sake. Through the years many had become so worn and soiled that in places they were no longer legible.

This Sampler contains more than 200 recipes specially selected from the original, beloved *Mennonite Community Cookbook* which contains more than 1,000 recipes the author has attempted to preserve for future generations. It is designed to give you only a "taste" of what wonderful country cooking is like. I hope it will make you want to add the original book to your cookbook collection.

Each Tuesday and Thursday evening Grandmother brought from the cellar or springhouse the can of liquid yeast that she had saved from the preceding bake day. She mixed into this some salt, sugar and fat and added enough warm water to make a gallon crock full of liquid. She then took the lid off the dough tray and at one end sifted a large amount of flour. Her next step was to make a well in the sifted flour and pour in the liquid. She worked the dough with her hands, adding more flour until she had a smooth, round ball of dough that no longer stuck to her fingers. Then she covered this with a clean cloth, put the lid on the tray, added another log to the fire, and went to bed.

In the morning she was up bright and early. As soon as breakfast had been started, she hurried to the outdoor oven in the back yard and made a fire. While the stones or bricks heated on the inside, she worked "out" the loaves

8

of bread. She usually had twelve to fourteen loaves each baking. When the oven had heated to the correct temperature, she raked all the coals and ashes outside and slipped in the pans of dough.

There are many families who still make all their own bread, but I know of none who continue to use the dough tray and outdoor oven. The dough tray has moved from the lowly corner in the kitchen to a place of distinction in someone's colonial-furnished living room. The outdoor oven, when seen at all, is covered with ivy and kept only for memory's sake.

Grandmother had other favorites that she made for holiday occasions or just to have variety. There was salt rising bread, which many of us still enjoy. It was made by setting a sponge of sliced potatoes, corn meal and hot water. This was allowed to stand overnight, and then flour was added. Cheese rolls, zwieback and Portzelky (yeast fritters) are favorites among the Russian Mennonites. The latter were always made at New Year's time.

Fried corn-meal mush for breakfast or a big dish of cooked mush and milk for supper was a good substitute for bread. Recently I learned a new way of making mush from an old recipe. It said, "Add enough meal and flour to the boiling water until it becomes sufficiently thick to say 'pouff' when it cooks!"

Breads

Chapter I

Basic White Bread Recipe

4 cups scalded milk or	2 tablespoons sugar
2 cups milk and 2 cups water	2 tablespoons salt
	3 tablespoons shortening
2 cakes compressed yeast	12 cups sifted flour

Dissolve yeast in ½ cup warm water.

Add fat, sugar and salt to scalded milk or boiling water.

Add softened yeast to milk that has cooled to lukewarm temperature.

Add flour gradually, making a dough stiff enough so that it can be easily handled.

Knead dough quickly and lightly until it is smooth and elastic.

Place in greased bowl, cover and set in a warm place to rise.

Let rise until double in bulk (about 2 hours).

Shape into loaves, brush with melted fat and allow to rise again until double in bulk.

Bake at 350-375° for approximately 1 hour or at 425° for 15 minutes and then reduce to 375° for 30 minutes.

When done, bread will shrink from the sides of the pan and should have a hollow sound when tapped.

When baked, remove bread from pans.

Do not cover while cooling if a crusty bread is desired.

Makes 3 large or 4 medium loaves.

Basic Roll Recipe

2 cups milk	¼ cup shortening
5 tablespoons sugar	1 yeast cake softened in ½
5-6 cups flour	cup warm water
1½ teaspoons salt	1 egg (optional)

Scald the milk and add shortening and sugar.

When liquid is cooled to lukewarm temperature, add yeast that has been dissolved in ½ cup lukewarm water.

Add 3 cups of flour and beat thoroughly.

Set sponge in a warm place for 30 minutes, or until light.

Beat egg and salt and add to sponge along with the remaining flour.

Knead until dough no longer sticks to the board or fingers.

When dough is light, cut into small pieces and shape into rolls.

Brush with fat and let rise until light.

Bake at 400-425° until a golden brown (15 to 20 minutes).

Makes approximately 2 dozen medium-sized rolls.

Foundation Sweet Dough Recipe

An Old Tried Recipe!

1 cup scalded milk	2 eggs, beaten
1 cup lukewarm water	7 cups flour
2 cakes compressed yeast	½ teaspoon nutmeg or
½ cup shortening	½ lemon, rind and juice
½ cup sugar	may be added
1½ teaspoons salt	

Scald milk and pour it over sugar, salt and shortening.
Dissolve yeast in lukewarm water.
Add beaten eggs.
When milk has cooled to lukewarm temperature, add the
  yeast and beaten eggs.
Beat well.
Add flour gradually, beating well.
Knead lightly, working in just enough flour so that dough
  can be handled.
Place dough in a greased bowl, cover and let stand in a
  warm place.
Let rise until double in bulk (about 2 hours).
Make into cinnamon, butterscotch or pecan rolls in fol-
  lowing recipes.

Whole Wheat Bread

An Old Recipe

1 cup scalded milk	¼ cup honey or syrup
1 cup hot water	3 tablespoons shortening
1 compressed yeast cake	2 cups white flour
1 tablespoon salt	4 cups whole wheat flour

Follow directions for basic white bread recipe (page 12).
Shape into loaves.
Bake at 350° for 50-60 minutes.
Makes 2 small-medium loaves.

Cinnamon Rolls

One recipe of foundation sweet dough.

6 tablespoons melted butter	1 tablespoon cinnamon
1½ cups brown sugar	1 cup raisins (optional)

When dough is light, divide into 2 portions.

Roll into oblong pieces ¼ inch thick.

Brush with melted butter and sprinkle with brown sugar and raisins.

Roll like a jelly roll and cut slices ½ inch thick, using a sharp knife.

Place slices 1 inch apart on greased tin with cut side down.

Let rise in a warm place until light (about 1 hour).

Bake at 400° for 20-25 minutes.

These may be spread with plain butter frosting while still warm.

They are also delicious if baked in 2 cups of syrup that is poured into the bottom of the pan before dough is added.

Another variation is to cut roll into ½ inch strips, but do not cut all the way through.

Then twine roll in a ring around the inside of a round pan and pour syrup over top to bake.

Orange Nut Bread

3 cups flour
1 teaspoon salt
4 teaspoons baking powder
¾ cup sugar
1 egg, beaten
1½ cups milk

1 teaspoon grated orange
peel
2 tablespoons melted
shortening
½ cup nuts, chopped

Sift flour; measure and add baking powder, salt and sugar.
  Sift again.
Combine milk, beaten egg and shortening and add to
  flour mixture.
Fold in orange peel and nuts.
Stir until mixed but do not beat.
Pour into a greased pan 4 x 8 inches.
Bake at 375° for 1 hour.
This makes delicious sandwiches when slices are spread
  with a filling made by adding chopped olives and pi-
  miento to cream cheese.

"Streusel Kuchen"
Raised Coffee Cake

2 cups milk
½ cup shortening
1 cup sugar
½ teaspoon salt
1 egg yolk

6½ cups flour
1 yeast cake (small)
¼ cup lukewarm water
1 egg white

Heat milk to boiling in top of double boiler and let it cool
  until lukewarm.
Cream together the butter, sugar, salt and egg yolk.

16

Add the yeast, which has been softened in ⅛ cup of luke-
warm water.
Add milk and flour alternately to above mixture.
Beat egg white until stiff and add to batter.
Allow to rise in a covered bowl overnight or until light.
Divide into 4 parts and pat each into a pie pan.
Let rise 1½ hours.
Sprinkle with streusel crumbs made with the following:

½ cup sugar	3 tablespoons soft butter
1 teaspoon cinnamon	½ teaspoon vanilla
¼ cup sifted flour	3 tablespoons chopped nuts

Bake at 425° for 20 minutes.

Dutch Apple Bread

2 cups flour	1 cup milk
3 teaspoons baking powder	2 tablespoons butter
2 tablespoons sugar	5 tart apples, pared and
1 teaspoon salt	sliced
1 egg	sugar and cinnamon

Sift flour; measure and add baking powder, salt and sugar.
Sift again.
Cut shortening into dry ingredients as for pastry.
Add beaten egg and milk.
Beat thoroughly until well blended.
Spread in a greased shallow pan, 8 x 12 inches.
Press apple slices over the top and sprinkle with sugar and
cinnamon.
Bake at 400° for 25-30 minutes.
Serve with milk.

Coffee Cake

Filling and topping:

½ cup brown sugar	2 tablespoons melted butter
2 teaspoons cinnamon	½ cup chopped nuts
2 tablespoons flour	¼ cup dates or raisins

Blend these ingredients together well before mixing coffee cake batter.

Coffee cake batter:

1½ cups sifted flour	¼ cup shortening
3 teaspoons baking powder	1 egg
¼ teaspoon salt	½ cup milk
¾ cup sugar	

Sift dry ingredients together and cut in shortening.
Beat egg well and add milk.
Combine liquid with dry ingredients.
Spread half the batter in a greased flat pan 8 x 8 inches or 6 x 10 inches.
Sprinkle with half of the filling.
Add the other half of the batter and sprinkle remaining filling on top.
Bake at 375° for 25 minutes.
Cut in squares.

Sour Cream Corn Bread
An Old Recipe

¾ cup corn meal	2½ tablespoons sugar
1 cup flour	1 egg, well beaten
1 teaspoon soda	2 tablespoons melted butter
1 teaspoon cream of tartar	1 cup thick sour cream
1 teaspoon salt	4 tablespoons milk

Sift flour and corn meal; measure and add soda, cream of
tartar, salt and sugar. Sift again.
Add beaten egg, cream, milk and melted shortening.
Beat thoroughly.
Pour into a greased pan 9 inches square.
Bake at 425° for 20 minutes.

Fastnachts or Raised Doughnuts

1¼ cups milk	3 eggs, beaten
¼ cup shortening	¾ cup sugar
1 teaspoon salt	¼ teaspoon nutmeg
1 small yeast cake	4½ to 5 cups sifted flour

Scald the milk, add shortening and salt.
Cool milk until it is lukewarm; then add crumbled yeast
cake and stir.
Gradually add 2⅝ cups sifted flour, beating batter
thoroughly.
Put in a warm place and allow to stand until full of bub-
bles.
Mix sugar with nutmeg and combine with beaten eggs.
Stir into first mixture and add remaining flour.
Knead well, cover and let rise in a warm place for about 1
hour.
Turn out lightly on floured board and roll ¾ inch thick.
Cut with doughnut cutter or biscuit cutter shaping into a
ball, or make into twists.
Cover with a thin cloth and let rise on board until top is
springy to touch of finger.
Drop into hot fat (375°) with the raised side down, so the
top side will rise while under side cooks.
Drain on absorbent paper.
Yields 3 dozen.

Buckwheat Griddle Cakes (With Yeast)

¼ yeast cake
¾ cup lukewarm water
1½ cups scalded milk
½ teaspoon salt

1¾ cups buckwheat flour
1 teaspoon baking soda
1 tablespoon molasses
1 egg

Soften yeast in ¼ cup water.
Scald milk and cool to lukewarm.
Stir in salt, yeast and flour.
Beat well.
Cover and let stand in a warm place overnight.
In the morning, dissolve soda in ½ cup warm water and
add to sponge.
Add molasses and beaten egg.
Bake on hot griddle.
Turn cakes only once.
Makes approximately 6-8 medium-sized cakes.

German Potato Pancakes

4 medium-sized potatoes
3 eggs
½ cup milk

1 teaspoon baking powder
½ cup flour
1 teaspoon salt

Pare the potatoes and grate them.
Add beaten eggs and sifted dry ingredients.
Drop from a spoon into a hot, greased frying pan.
Bake until a golden brown on both sides.
Makes 10-12 cakes.

Soups

Chapter II

Bean Soup with Pork

1½ pounds ham butt
1 pound soup beans
1 cup diced celery
2 onions, chopped
2 cups strained tomatoes or tomato juice
2 teaspoons minced parsley
Salt and pepper

Soak beans overnight in enough water to cover.
In the morning drain and add 2 quarts of fresh water, cook until almost tender.
Wash ham, cover with cold water and cook until tender.
Skim fat from the broth and add beans.
Add other ingredients, season, and cook until vegetables are soft.
Serves 8.

Borsch

Russian Vegetable Soup

2 pounds beef (with soup bone)
2 carrots
1 medium-sized head of cabbage
2 medium-sized onions
2 cups fresh or canned tomatoes
6 medium-sized potatoes
6 whole pepper kernels
1 bay leaf
A few sprigs of parsley or dill
½ cup sour cream
1 cup chopped beets (optional)

Cover meat with cold water and bring to a boil.
Let simmer until almost tender, adding water if necessary to keep meat covered.
One hour before serving, add chopped vegetables and seasonings.

Potatoes may be cooked separately and added just before serving.

When ready to serve, remove from heat and add sour cream.

This is a delicious thick soup.

Serves 8.

Chicken and Corn Soup

1 chicken (preferably a 4-pound hen)	2½ cups fresh or frozen corn
4 quarts of cold water	2 cooked eggs (optional)
1 onion, chopped	Salt and pepper
½ cup chopped celery and leaves	

Cook chicken slowly until it is tender, adding salt 30 minutes before it is done.

Remove chicken and strain broth through a fine sieve.

Take meat from bones and cut in bite sized pieces. Set aside.

Add corn to broth and bring to boil.

Add chopped celery and seasoning and cook 5 minutes.

Five minutes before serving, add chicken, diced eggs, and rivels made from:

1 cup flour	¼ cup milk
1 egg	

Rub this mixture together with 2 forks until the size of peas and drop into boiling soup.

Cover and cook gently for 5 minutes.

Serves 10. This is delicious!

Corn Chowder

4 slices bacon	3 tomatoes
1 tablespoon minced celery	2 cups corn
1 tablespoon minced pepper	2 pints milk
1 tablespoon minced onion	Salt and pepper
2 potatoes, diced	

Chop bacon and place in pan to brown.
Add minced celery, pepper and onion.
Fry together until bacon is brown.
Add corn and sauté together for 3 minutes.
Add the chopped vegetables including diced potatoes and
1 cup of water.
Cover and cook slowly for 30 minutes.
Then add rich milk, and heat to boiling again.
Add chopped parsley.
Serves 4.

Old-fashioned Potato Soup

With Dry Rivels

4 medium-sized potatoes	½ cup flour
1½ quarts water	1 egg
2 tablespoons butter	¼ cup milk
Salt	½ cup cream

Cook diced potatoes in salt water until soft. Add butter.
To make rivels, rub egg and flour together, then add milk.
These are best made by cutting through mixture with two
forks.
Drop rivels, which are no larger than a cherry stone, into
boiling potatoes, stirring to prevent packing together.
Cook 5 minutes with kettle covered.
Add ½ cup cream.
Garnish with parsley or pieces of crisp bacon.
Serves 4.

Beef Soup with Dumplings

1 soup bone with 2 pounds stewing beef	1½ cups flour
2 quarts water	1 egg
Salt	½ cup milk

Cook meat until tender and remove from broth.
Add water until you have 2 quarts of broth.
Make dumplings by mixing beaten egg and milk into flour to form a batter the consistency of pancake batter.
Drop from a teaspoon into boiling broth.
Cook 8 minutes with cover on the kettle.
Serves 8.

Cream of Tomato Soup

3 tablespoons butter or fat	¼ teaspoon celery salt
2½ tablespoons flour	1 tablespoon sugar
3 cups strained tomatoes or tomato juice	2 teaspoons salt
	1 quart milk
1 tablespoon minced onion	⅛ teaspoon pepper

Melt butter in top of double boiler.
Add flour, salt, pepper and celery salt.
Add milk gradually and stir until thickened.
In a separate pan heat tomatoes and minced onion.
Cook until onion is soft and then strain.
Add tomatoes to milk slowly and stir.
If milk and tomatoes are both near boiling point and tomatoes are added slowly, this will not curd.
Should it curd, beat briskly with an egg beater.
Serves 6.

Oyster Stew

1 quart milk	⅛ teaspoon pepper
1 pint oysters	1 tablespoon minced
2 tablespoons butter	parsley or celery leaves
1 teaspoon salt	

Bring milk to a boil in the top of a double boiler. Add salt.
Melt the butter in a saucepan.
Drain oysters and add one at a time to the butter.
When both the oysters in the butter and the milk are at the
boiling point, pour oysters into milk.
Add minced parsley or celery leaves and serve at once.
Serves 6.

Pflaumenus

"Pluma Moos"

1½ cups raisins	½ cup flour
1 cup dried prunes	¼ cup sugar
½ cup sugar	½ teaspoon salt
3 pints water	3 cups milk

Add water to dried fruits and cook until almost soft. Add
½ cup sugar during the last 5 minutes of the cooking
period.
Make a paste of the milk, flour, salt and ¼ cup sugar.
Add thickening to fruit and stir until done.
If soup seems too thick, add more milk or a small amount
of water.

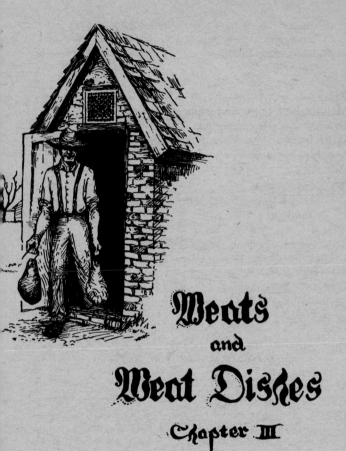

Meats
and
Meat Dishes
Chapter III

Beef and Biscuit

1 pound ground beef
½ cup finely chopped onion
½ cup chopped green
  pepper
1 teaspoon salt

⅛ teaspoon pepper
2 tablespoons shortening
2 tablespoons flour
1 cup milk or water

Brown meat, onion and pepper in hot fat.
Season with salt and pepper.
Add flour and blend, then add liquid and cook until thick.
For biscuit dough:

2 cups flour
4 teaspoons baking powder
1 teaspoon salt

3 tablespoons shortening
¾ cup milk

Roll biscuit dough ¼ inch thick, brush with melted butter
  and spread with meat mixture.
Roll like a jelly roll and cut in 1¼ inch slices.
Place cut slices down in a greased baking pan.
Bake at 400° for 20 to 25 minutes.
Serves 6-8.

Old-fashioned Beef Potpie

2 pounds stewing beef
6 cups water
1½ teaspoons salt
4 medium-sized potatoes
1½ cups flour

1 egg
3 tablespoons milk or
  water
1 teaspoon minced onion
1 teaspoon minced parsley

Cook meat in salt water until it is tender.
Remove meat from broth; add minced onion and parsley
  to broth.
Bring to boiling point and add alternate layers of cubed
  potatoes and squares of dough.

28

To make potpie dough, beat egg and add milk.
Add flour to make a stiff dough.
Roll out paper-thin and cut in inch squares.
Keep broth boiling while adding dough squares in order to keep them from packing together.
Cover and cook for 20 minutes, adding more water if needed.
Add meat and stir through potpie.
Serves 6 to 8.

Browned Stew with Dumplings

2 pounds cubed beef	1½ teaspoons salt
2 tablespoons flour	⅛ teaspoon pepper
3 tablespoons fat	1 quart boiling water
1 small onion	1 teaspoon lemon juice

Cut meat into small cubes.
Melt fat in hot skillet or Dutch oven.
Brown meat in fat, keep it sizzling hot until nicely browned.
Sprinkle flour, salt and pepper over meat.
Add the boiling water.
Cover the pan and lower heat so that meat simmers for 3 to 3½ hours.
One teaspoon lemon juice added at the same time the water is added improves flavor and tenderizes meat.
To make dumplings take:

1 cup flour	1 egg
1½ teaspoons baking powder	2 to 3 tablespoons milk
½ teaspoon salt	1 tablespoon shortening

Stir quickly and drop from a spoon on simmering stew.
Cover and allow to cook 12 to 15 minutes. Delicious!
Serves 6-8.

Barbecued Hamburger

2 pounds hamburger
1 onion
½ cup catsup
2 tablespoons brown sugar
2 tablespoons vinegar

2 teaspoons prepared mustard
1 teaspoon Worcestershire sauce
1 teaspoon salt

Fry onion and hamburger in 4 tablespoons hot fat until it has lost its raw, red color.
Stir until smooth and then add all the other ingredients.
Simmer about 20 minutes and serve with hamburger rolls.
Serves 8.

Steak and Onion Pie

1 cup onions, sliced
¼ cup shortening
1 pound round steak, cubed
¼ cup flour
2 teaspoons salt

½ teaspoon pepper
½ teaspoon paprika
2 cups raw potatoes, diced
2½ cups boiling water
Pastry for 1 crust

Cook onions slowly in melted fat. Remove onions.
Roll meat in mixture of flour and seasoning.
Brown meat in hot fat.
Add boiling water, cover and simmer 1 hour.
Add potatoes and cook 10 minutes longer.
Pour into greased casserole, lay cooked onions on top.
Cover with crust rolled ¼ inch thick.
Bake at 400° for 30-35 minutes.
Serves 6-8.

Meat Loaf

1½ pounds hamburger	1 or 2 eggs, beaten
1 cup soft bread crumbs	1 teaspoon salt
1 cup milk or tomato juice	⅛ teaspoon pepper
1 medium-sized onion, minced	6 strips bacon

Soak crumbs in milk and add beaten egg.
Add meat, onion and seasoning.
Form into a loaf (do not pack) and place in baking dish; then put strips of bacon on top of loaf.
Bake at 375° for 1 hour.
Serves 6.

This mixture may also be shaped in individual servings and placed in greased muffin tins.
Spread top with a sauce made by combining the following:

3 tablespoons brown sugar	1 teaspoon dry mustard
¼ cup catsup	

Another variation may be made by removing baked hamburger loaf from pan and placing it in a broiler pan.
Spread with catsup and place under broiler for several minutes.

Horse-radish dressing is good served with meat loaf.
Take:

¼ cup thick cream	¼ teaspoon salt
3 tablespoons grated horse-radish	1 tablespoon vinegar

Mix vinegar and salt with grated horse-radish.
Whip the cream stiff and add gradually to horse-radish.

Old-fashioned Hash

3 cups leftover roast meat   1½ teaspoons salt
1 cup mashed potatoes   1½ cups milk
1 medium-sized onion   ½ cup bread crumbs

Grind meat and onion in food chopper.
Add mashed potatoes, salt and milk. Mix well.
Place in a casserole and sprinkle crumbs over top.
Bake at 350° for 30 minutes.
Serves 6.

Roasted Pig's Stomach
Dutch Goose

1 pig stomach   2 cups shredded cabbage
1½ pounds ground sausage   2 tablespoons salt
1 quart diced potatoes, raw   1 teaspoon pepper
1 onion, chopped fine

Remove the inner lining of the stomach and discard.
Wash stomach well and then soak in salt water several
    hours.
Drain and fill stomach with stuffing. Sew securely.

Use either of the following recipes for the filling.

I
Make a filling of raw diced potatoes, chopped onion and
    shredded cabbage.
Add seasoning and mix well.

II
Make a bread filling by browning diced onion and bread
    cubes in butter.

Mix with egg, parsley, and milk.

Stir in diced boiled potatoes and 1 pound sausage. Mix thoroughly.

Place stuffed stomach on a rack in a kettle, cover with water and cook slowly until tender.

Then brown in a hot pan to which butter has been added.

Or

Place stuffed stomach in a roasting pan and bake at 350° for approximately 3 hours.

Serve with gravy made by adding flour and water to drippings in roasting pan.

Serves 8 to 10.

Scrapple

1½ cups liver pudding or sausage	1 cup corn meal
3 quarts broth from cooked pudding	3 cups whole wheat flour
	1½ teaspoons salt
	½ teaspoon pepper

Bring to a boil broth in which pudding meat was cooked.

Season with salt and pepper.

Stir into the boiling broth the corn meal and flour.

Add ground liver pudding.

This should be the consistency of corn meal mush.

Cook slowly in heavy pan or top of double boiler for approximately 30 minutes.

Pour in dishes to mold.

When cold, slice ¼ inch thick and fry in hot fat until brown and crusty on both sides.

Meat Pie

1½ cups leftover meat	½ teaspoon salt
3 tablespoons flour	⅛ teaspoon pepper
¼ cup broth or drippings	2 teaspoons grated onion
1 cup milk	⅓ cup chopped pepper

Add flour to drippings and stir until blended.
Add milk and cook until thickened.
Add salt, minced onion and green peppers.
Stir meat into gravy and pour into pastry-lined dish.
Cover top with pastry (page 94).
Bake at 425° for 25 minutes.
Serves 6.

Pigs in the Blanket

1 pound hamburger	¼ teaspoon pepper
¾ cup tomato juice	½ teaspoon Worcestershire
1 small onion, minced	sauce
1 teaspoon salt	

Make your favorite biscuit dough.
Roll to ¼ inch thickness and cut into 4 inch squares.
Place one tablespoon meat mixture in center of each
  square.
Fold over dough so meat is covered.
Place in pan and bake at 425° for 40 minutes.
Makes 8 "pigs."

Baked Ham

2 slices ham, ¾ to 1 inch thick	1 teaspoon dry mustard
4 tablespoons brown sugar	Milk to cover

Cut slices of meat through center of cured ham.

Place in a large skillet or Dutch oven.
Rub with dry mustard and cover with brown sugar.
Add enough milk to barely cover ham.
Bake at 325° for 1 to 1¼ hours.
Milk should be absorbed.
This is delicious!
Serves 8 to 10.

Snitz and Knepp

1½ pounds cured ham or 1 ham hock	2 cups dried apples
	2 tablespoons brown sugar

Wash dried apples, cover with water and soak overnight.
In the morning, cover ham with cold water and cook slowly for 3 hours.
Add apples and water in which they soaked.
Add brown sugar and cook 1 hour longer.

For knepp or dumplings:

2 cups flour	1 egg, beaten
3½ teaspoons baking powder	2 tablespoons butter
½ teaspoon salt	⅓ to ½ cup milk

Sift together dry ingredients.
Stir in beaten egg and melted butter.
Add milk to make a batter stiff enough to drop from a spoon.
Drop batter by spoonfuls into boiling ham and apples.
Cover pan tightly and cook dumplings 10 to 12 minutes.
Do not lift cover until ready to serve.
Serves 8.

Baked Sausage Pie

1 pound fresh sausage
4 cups diced cooked
    potatoes
2 onions, minced
½ cup diced celery
1 tablespoon chopped
    parsley

1½ teaspoons salt
⅛ teaspoon pepper
Milk to cover mixture
Pastry for bottom and top
    crust (page 94)

Line the bottom and sides of a flat baking dish with pas-
    try.
Fill dish with alternate layers of fresh sausage and cooked,
    diced potatoes.
Add onion, celery and seasoning.
Cover mixture with hot milk and add top crust.
Bake at 350° for 1 hour.
Serves 6-8.

Ham Rolls with Cheese Sauce

2 cups flour
4 teaspoons baking powder
½ teaspoon salt
4 tablespoons fat
¾ cup milk

1 cup ground cooked ham
2 tablespoons soft butter
1½ tablespoons prepared
    mustard

Add butter and mustard to the ground ham.
Sift together flour, baking powder and salt and cut in fat.
Add milk to make a soft dough.
Roll out dough ¼ inch thick and spread with ham mixture.
Roll as a jelly roll and cut into slices 1½ inches thick.
Place cut side down in a greased pan and bake at 425° for
    15 to 20 minutes.
When baked, serve with cheese sauce (page 47).
Serves 6.

Poultry and Fish

Chapter IV

Chicken a la King

2 tablespoons butter
1 teaspoon minced onion
½ cup flour
3½ cups chicken stock
3 cups diced cooked chicken
1½ teaspoons salt
¼ teaspoon pepper

¾ cup milk
⅓ cup chopped green pepper
⅓ cup red pimiento, chopped
1 cup chopped mushrooms, cooked
2 egg yolks

Sauté onion and green pepper in hot butter until slightly browned.
Remove from fat.
Add flour and blend into fat.
Add stock and cook until thickened.
Then add chopped chicken, cooked mushrooms and seasoning.
Heat together thoroughly.
Beat egg yolks and add milk.
Stir this into chicken and stir until blended. Add pimiento.
Remove from heat and serve.
Serves 8.

Chicken and Dumplings

1 chicken, a year-old hen preferred
1½ teaspoons salt
Water to cover
3 medium-sized potatoes
1 small onion
2 tablespoons chopped parsley

For dumplings:
1½ cups flour
½ teaspoon salt
3 teaspoons baking powder
1 egg
2 to 3 tablespoons milk

Cut chicken into serving pieces.
Cover with water and cook slowly until almost tender.

Add sliced potatoes and finely chopped onion, parsley and
seasoning.
Cook 15 more minutes and then add the dumplings to the
boiling broth and meat.
To make dumplings, sift dry ingredients together.
Add beaten egg and milk. Stir until well blended.
The dough should be stiff enough to drop from a spoon.
Drop dough from a teaspoon into boiling chicken.
Cover tightly and cook 10 more minutes.
Do not uncover until ready to serve.
Serves 6 to 8.

Fried Chicken

3½ pound fryer	2 teaspoons salt
½ cup flour	⅛ teaspoon pepper

Cut chicken into serving pieces.
Wash pieces of chicken, drain but do not wipe dry.
Sprinkle well with salt and pepper mixture.
Place flour in paper bag and dredge pieces with flour by
shaking them in bag until well covered.
Melt fat to a depth of ½ inch in a heavy skillet.
When fat is moderately hot, add pieces of chicken.
Do not crowd them in pan.
Turn the pieces to brown them on all sides.
If a crisp crust is desired, cover the pan for the first half
hour of the cooking period, then uncover.
If a tender crust is desired, brown pieces with pan un-
covered and then remove them to rack in roasting pan.
Cover and bake at 325° for 1 hour or in electric skillet for
30-40 minutes.
If desired, a pressure saucepan may be used for steaming
after chicken has been fried a golden brown.
Serves 6.

Parsley Pinwheel Potpie

1 chicken or 2½-pound
  piece of beef
1 teaspoon salt
Water to cover
4 medium-sized potatoes
2 tablespoons chopped
  parsley

For potpie:
2 cups flour
1 teaspoon salt
3 teaspoons baking powder
4 tablespoons shortening
½ cup milk (approximate)

To make potpie follow procedure for pastry (page 94).
Roll pastry dough in an oblong shape ⅛ inch thick.
Spread parsley over the dough and roll as a jelly roll.
Cut in 1½ to 2 inch lengths.
Place cooked pieces of chicken in a casserole, then add a
  layer of sliced raw potatoes.
Make a gravy of the chicken stock and pour it over the
  mixture in the casserole; have enough to cover.
Place pieces of dough on top of casserole with cut side
  down.
Bake at 425° for 25 minutes.
Serves 6-8.

Baked Chicken Potpie

1 chicken, preferably a
  4-pound hen
1 teaspoon salt
Water to cover
4 medium-sized potatoes
Parsley

For potpie dough:
2 cups flour
½ teaspoon salt
⅓ cup shortening
1 teaspoon baking powder
½ cup milk

Cook the chicken in salt water and remove the meat from the bones.

Leave meat in as large pieces as possible.

Make pastry and line the bottom and sides of a baking dish.

Sprinkle with salt, pepper, parsley and minced onion.

Add pieces of chicken, then a layer of sliced potatoes.

Add another layer of chicken and potatoes.

Pour broth over mixture and place a pastry lid on top.

Cut holes in the lid to keep liquid from cooking out. Fasten edges securely.

Bake at 350° for 1 hour.

This is delicious.

Serves 6-8.

Fried Bread Stuffing

1 loaf bread	1½ teaspoons salt
2 cups mashed potatoes	⅛ teaspoon saffron
3 eggs	1 minced onion or
3 cups milk	¼ cup celery if desired
3 tablespoons chicken fat or butter	

Beat eggs, add milk and pour over bread crumbs.

Add mashed potatoes and seasoning and mix together.

Melt 3 tablespoons of chicken fat or butter in a pan and add the mixture.

Let it simmer on top of the stove for 15 minutes.

Fill chicken while dressing is hot.

Baked Stuffed Fish

3 to 4 pounds, shad, rock
    or other large fish
2 teaspoons salt
2 onions

6 medium-sized potatoes
4 to 5 strips of bacon
1 cup hot water

Clean fish and leave whole.

Rub salt on the inside and outside.

Place in a roasting pan.

Cut onion and potatoes into rather thick slices and lay these around the edge and inside of the fish.

Sprinkle vegetables with salt.

Lay strips of bacon on top of the fish.

Add hot water and bake at 375° for approximately 1¼ hours.

Serves 6 to 8.

Oyster Pie

1 pint oysters
1 teaspoon salt
4 medium-sized potatoes
    (or 2 cups crushed
    crackers)
¼ teaspoon pepper

1 tablespoon minced
    parsley
1½ cups milk
Pastry for two crusts
    (page 94)

Line flat baking dish with pastry.

Arrange alternate layers of oysters and sliced potatoes or crushed crackers in a greased casserole.

Season with salt, pepper and parsley.

Add milk and oyster liquor.

Place a crust over top and bake at 375° for 45 minutes.

Serves 6.

Cheese,
Egg and Casserole Dishes

Chapter V

Soda Cheese

1 gallon sour milk	1 teaspoon salt
½ teaspoon soda	1 cup cream
3 tablespoons butter	1 egg, beaten

Heat sour milk to 115°.

Cut through it both ways with a knife to aid in heating.

Pour into a cloth bag and let stand overnight to drain thoroughly.

When dry, crumble cheese and stir in soda and butter.

Let stand 5 hours.

Place in a double boiler and allow it to melt.

Add cream and stir until smooth.

Add salt and beaten egg and butter coloring.

Let come to a boil and then pour into a dish.

Cheese Fondue

6 slices of bread ½ inch thick	3 eggs
1 cup grated American cheese	2½ cups milk
	½ teaspoon salt

Cut bread in cubes and place in the bottom of a greased, shallow baking dish.

Sprinkle with grated cheese.

Beat eggs, add milk and salt.

Pour liquid over bread and cheese.

Let stand 30 minutes.

Set in a pan of hot water and bake at 350° for 40 minutes.

This is delicious if sliced and served with creamed ham.

Serves 6-8.

Eggs in Ham Nests

1¾ cups cooked ground ham
2 tablespoons ham fat
2 tablespoons flour
¼ teaspoon salt

1 teaspoon dry mustard
1 cup milk
6 eggs

Melt fat, add flour and blend.

Add chopped ham and cook 2 minutes, stirring constantly.

Add salt, mustard and milk and cook slowly until thickened.

Pour into a greased shallow baking dish.

Make 6 hollows in the mixture and drop an egg into each.

Sprinkle with salt and pepper.

Bake at 325° for 25 minutes or until firm.

Serves 6.

Baked Macaroni and Cheese

2 cups macaroni
6 cups boiling water
1 teaspoon salt
2 tablespoons butter

1 tablespoon flour
1½ cups milk
1½ cups grated cheese
½ cup bread crumbs

Cook macaroni in salt water and drain.

Make a white sauce of fat, flour and milk.

Place a layer of macaroni in the bottom of a greased casserole.

Add grated cheese and white sauce.

Repeat until the casserole is filled.

Sprinkle crumbs over the top and bake at 375° for 30 minutes.

Serves 6.

Baked Noodles and Tuna with Mushrooms

⅓ pound noodles
1½ quarts boiling water
1½ teaspoons salt
1 cup canned tuna

One 10½ oz. can mushroom
soup
¼ cup buttered crumbs

Cook noodles in salt water until tender and drain.
Flake the tuna with a fork.
Mix with noodles and mushroom soup.
Turn into a greased baking dish.
Sprinkle with crumbs and bake at 350° for 40 minutes.
Serves 6.

Cheese and Noodle Ring

3 cups medium-wide
noodles
½ pound processed cheese
1 cup hot milk

2 tablespoons butter
1 teaspoon salt
½ teaspoon paprika
4 eggs, separated

Cook the noodles in salt water until tender.
Drain and rinse with cold water.
Melt the cheese in the hot milk, add butter, salt and
paprika.
Add to noodles and then fold in beaten egg yolks.
Beat egg whites until stiff and fold in gently.
Pour into a greased and chilled ring mold.
Place mold in a pan of hot water and bake at 350° for 45
minutes.
Serves 6-8.

Cheese Sauce

3 tablespoons shortening
   (butter preferred)
2 tablespoons flour
1 teaspoon salt

2 cups milk
⅛ teaspoon pepper
   (optional)
1½ cups grated cheese

Melt shortening over low heat. Add flour and seasoning.
Stir until well blended.
Gradually add milk, stirring constantly.
Cook until thick and smooth.
Add grated cheese and stir until it is melted.
Serve with meat, vegetables and casserole dishes.
Makes 2½ cups.

Rice Ring

1 cup uncooked rice
1½ quarts water

1½ teaspoons salt
3 tablespoons butter

Cook rice in salt water until soft. Drain.
Add melted butter and mix thoroughly.
Press rice into a buttered ring mold and set in a pan of hot
   water for 20 minutes or until rice has heated thoroughly.
Unmold on a platter and fill the center with creamed salm-
   on or creamed chicken to which chopped olives have
   been added.
Serves 6-8.

Spatzlein (Little Sparrows)

1 egg	2 quarts boiling water
1 cup water	1½ teaspoons salt
2½ cups flour	

Beat egg thoroughly.

Add water and beat until well blended with egg.

Add flour and beat until smooth.

Bring salt water to a boil and drop spatzlein into water.

To do this, tilt bowl containing batter in a position that it can be cut with the edge of a spoon as it pours over edge of bowl.

The spatzlein should be an inch long and ¼ inch in diameter.

Cook for 3 minutes after batter is all in the water.

Drain in colander and top with brown butter.

Makes 6 servings.

Homemade Noodles

1½ cups flour	3 tablespoons water
1 teaspoon salt	1 egg
1 teaspoon fat	

Make a well in the flour and add egg, salt and fat.

Rub together and add water to form a stiff dough. Knead.

Divide dough into three parts and roll each as thin as possible.

Spread rolled dough on a cloth and allow to dry partially.

Then cut dough into strips about 1½ inches wide and stack on top of each other. Then cut crosswise into fine shreds.

Or you may roll dough as a jelly roll and cut into fine shreds.

These are then ready to use like packaged noodles.

Vegetables
and
Vegetable Dishes

Chapter VI

Baked Acorn Squash

3 acorn squash	1 teaspoon salt
6 tablespoons honey or syrup	1 pound pork sausage
	1 teaspoon sage

Wash each squash and cut in half.

Remove seeds and strings.

Put a tablespoon of honey or syrup in each half and sprinkle with salt and powdered sage.

Fill the cavity with pork sausage and top with bread crumbs.

Place halves in baking pan and add about 1 inch of water.

Cover and bake at 400° for 40 minutes.

Remove cover and allow to brown.

Serves 6.

Baked Beans

4 cups navy beans	2 teaspoons mustard
3 teaspoons salt	¼ teaspoon ginger
1 onion, minced	½ cup catsup
½ cup molasses	½ pound salt pork or bacon

Soak beans overnight in cold water.

Drain and add 2½ quarts fresh water and minced onion.

Cook slowly until the skins burst.

Drain and save liquid.

Mix molasses, seasoning and catsup.

Add 2 cups of liquid from the beans.

Place a piece of pork in the bottom of the bean jar or baking dish.

Add the beans and place the remaining pork on top.

Pour molasses mixture over beans.

Add enough water to cover.

Bake with cover on for 5 hours at 300°.

Remove cover the last 30 minutes.

Add water as necessary during cooking process.

Serves 10.

Schnitzel Beans

4 slices of bacon or ¼ pound cubed ham
3 medium-sized onions, sliced
1 quart string beans

2 cups tomatoes
1 teaspoon salt
¼ teaspoon pepper
⅓ cup boiling water

Dice bacon or ham and fry until crisp.
Add sliced onions and fry until a light brown.
Then add string beans that have been cut into small pieces and brown slightly.
Add tomatoes, seasoning and boiling water.
Cover and cook until beans are tender.
Serves 6.

Sauerkraut with Spareribs and Dumplings

1 quart sauerkraut
2 teaspoons sugar

1½ pounds spareribs

Cook spareribs in sufficient water to cover until almost tender.
Add kraut and continue to cook for 30 minutes.
Add sugar if desired.
To make dumplings:

1½ cups flour
½ teaspoon salt
3 teaspoons baking powder
1 egg, beaten

¼ to ⅓ cup milk
1 tablespoon melted butter or margarine

Mix ingredients together to make a stiff dough.
Drop from a spoon onto the boiling kraut.
Cook 10 to 12 minutes in tightly covered pan.
Serves 6 to 8.

Cabbage Bundles or Stuffed Cabbage Leaves
Golubtzi

1 large head of cabbage	1 teaspoon salt
½ pound hamburger or chopped round steak	¼ teaspoon pepper
1 cup rice, cooked	One 10½ oz. can tomato soup
1 onion, minced	½ cup sour cream
2 tablespoons fat	

Remove outer leaves from the cabbage head and cook in salt water for about 5 minutes, or until leaves are flexible.

Drain and cool.

Add minced onion to 2 tablespoons of fat and brown slightly.

Add ground meat, cooked rice, and seasoning.

Drop a tablespoon of the mixture on the stem end of each cabbage leaf.

Start rolling from the rib end and tie securely with thread or fasten with toothpicks.

Place bundles in a baking pan and pour undiluted tomato soup over them.

Bake at 350° for 45 minutes or simmer slowly on top of the stove until tender.

Add sour cream 5 minutes before serving.

Serves 6.

Hot Slaw

1 quart shredded cabbage	½ cup water
1 teaspoon salt	2 tablespoons butter
2 tablespoons sugar	½ teaspoon mustard
2 tablespoons vinegar	½ cup sour cream

Melt butter in a saucepan and add shredded cabbage.

Stir until butter is well mixed through the cabbage.

Add water and salt and cover tightly.

Cook for 10 minutes and then add the sugar, vinegar and mustard.
Simmer another minute and then add the sour cream.
Serves 4.

Cooked Celery with Sweet-Sour Dressing

2 cups diced celery	2 tablespoons flour
1 teaspoon salt	1 egg
2 tablespoons sugar	1 cup water
1½-2 tablespoons vinegar	¼ cup sour cream

Cut celery in 1 inch pieces; the outside stems may be used.
Cook celery in salt water until tender and almost dry.
Make a dressing with the egg, flour, sugar, vinegar and water.
Bring dressing to a boil; when it thickens add the sour cream.
Pour dressing over the celery and serve at once.
Serves 5.

Baked Corn

2 cups cooked or canned corn	1 tablespoon sugar
2 tablespoons fat	1 teaspoon salt
1½ tablespoons flour	⅛ teaspoon pepper
1 cup milk	2 eggs
	½ cup buttered crumbs

Melt the fat and add the flour.
Add milk gradually and bring to the boiling point, stirring constantly.
Add corn, sugar, salt and pepper and heat thoroughly.
Remove from heat and add beaten eggs.
Pour in a greased baking dish and sprinkle with buttered crumbs. Bake at 350° for 35 minutes or until corn is firm.
Serves 4.

Corn Fritters

2 cups fresh corn, grated	⅛ teaspoon pepper
2 eggs	1 teaspoon baking powder
¼ cup flour	2 tablespoons cream
1 teaspoon salt	4 tablespoons fat

Add beaten eggs, flour, baking powder, salt and pepper to the grated corn. Mix thoroughly. Add the cream.

Melt the fat in a frying pan and drop corn mixture by spoonfuls into the hot fat. Brown on both sides.

Makes 16-18 fritters.

Fried Tomatoes

4 medium-sized tomatoes	⅛ teaspoon pepper
½ cup flour	2 tablespoons brown sugar
½ teaspoon salt	1 cup cream
3 tablespoons fat	

Use ripe but firm tomatoes.

Do not remove skins.

Cut in slices ⅛ inch thick.

Roll in flour and fry in hot fat.

When browned on both sides, sprinkle with salt, pepper and brown sugar.

Place tomatoes on a platter.

Add 1 tablespoon flour to fryings; when well blended add the cream.

Allow gravy to thicken and then pour it over the fried tomatoes.

Serves 5.

Creamed Mushrooms

2 pounds mushrooms
½ cup butter
½ cup water
½ teaspoon salt
⅛ teaspoon pepper
½ cup flour
3 cups milk

To clean mushrooms, pull caps from stems.
If young and tender, do not pare caps, brush them well.
Put the butter and water in a heavy saucepan or skillet.
Add cleaned mushroom caps and stems, salt and pepper.
Cover and steam slowly for 20 minutes or until dry.
Allow to brown slightly and then add flour.
Brown the flour, watching it carefully.
Add milk gradually and stir until thickened.
Serves 8.

Baked Peppers

With Hamburger or Sausage

4 large green peppers
½ pound sausage or
hamburger
1 cup canned or fresh corn
or Lima beans
½ cup crushed soda
crackers
½ teaspoon salt
⅛ teaspoon pepper

Cut peppers in half lengthwise; remove seeds and veins.
Parboil for 5 minutes and allow to cool.
Brown meat slightly and mix meat, corn or Lima beans
    and seasoning.
Fill pepper halves and top with cracker crumbs.
Arrange in a greased baking dish.
Bake at 375° for 25 minutes.
Serves 6 to 8.

Sweet Potato Balls or Croquettes

2 cups mashed sweet
  potatoes
1 teaspoon salt
1½ tablespoons butter

1 tablespoon sugar
6 marshmallows
1½ cups crushed corn flakes
1 egg white

Cook sweet potatoes until soft; then mash very fine.
Season mashed sweet potatoes with salt, sugar and melted
  butter.
Shape potato mixture around a marshmallow.
Chill in refrigerator 30 minutes.
Dip balls into slightly beaten egg white and roll in corn
  flakes.
Place in a flat, greased baking dish and bake at 400° for
  20 minutes or until golden brown.
Serves 6.

Baked Salsify

2 cups cooked salsify
  (oyster plant)
2 eggs
3 cups crushed soda
  crackers

2 tablespoons butter
1½ teaspoons salt
⅛ teaspoon pepper
3 cups milk

Clean salsify and cut in small pieces.
Cook in salt water until tender.
Break crackers in small pieces and place a layer in a
  greased baking dish.
Add a layer of salsify and sprinkle with salt and pepper.
Continue to add alternate layers until the contents are used.
Have cracker crumbs on top.
Beat eggs and add milk.
Pour this over ingredients.
Dot with butter.
Bake at 350° for 35 minutes.
Serves 6.

Salads

and

Salad Dressings

Chapter VII.

Bean Salad

3 cups cooked navy or
  string beans
4 hard-cooked eggs
1 medium-sized onion
1 large sour pickle,
  chopped

2 tablespoons vinegar
1½ teaspoons salt
⅔ cup salad dressing

Chop eggs, onion and pickle.
If green string beans are used, cut in 1 inch lengths.
Add beans and seasoning.
Mix together and add salad dressing.
Serves 8.

Beet Salad

Dressing:

6 small beets, cooked
1 medium-sized onion,
  diced
1½ cups shredded cabbage

1 egg, beaten
2 teaspoons sugar
1 teaspoon mustard
1 teaspoon salt
1 tablespoon flour
¼ cup vinegar
1 cup sour cream

Cook beets, peel and dice.
Mix with onion and cabbage.
Mix together the ingredients for the dressing. See directions for Cooked Salad Dressing (page 64).
Cook until thickened; then pour sauce over the vegetables.
Stir until well blended.
Serves 6.

Cole Slaw

4 cups finely shredded cabbage	3 tablespoons sugar
¼ cup sour cream	1 teaspoon salt
¼ cup vinegar	⅛ teaspoon mustard

Chop or shred the cabbage.
Mix together the sugar, salt, mustard, vinegar and sour cream.
Pour over cabbage and mix well.
Garnish with green pepper rings.
Serves 6.

Dandelion Salad

Dressing:

4 cups chopped dandelion	1½ tablespoons flour
3 hard-cooked eggs	1 teaspoon salt
3 slices bacon	1 egg
	2 tablespoons sugar
	¼ cup vinegar
	2 cups milk or water

Wash and chop dandelion.
Cut bacon in pieces and fry until crisp.
Remove bacon from drippings.
To make dressing, mix together the dry ingredients, add egg, vinegar and water. Stir until well blended.
Cook in bacon drippings until thickened and cool slightly.
Pour dressing over dandelion and mix lightly. Garnish with sliced or chopped eggs and the crisp bacon.
Serves 6.

Potato Salad

	Dressing:
8 medium-sized potatoes	1 tablespoon flour
4 hard-cooked eggs	2 eggs
1 medium-sized onion	½ cup sugar
2 small carrots, ground	½ cup vinegar
1 cup celery, diced	1 teaspoon mustard
1½ teaspoons salt	1½ cups water
	2 tablespoons butter

Cook potatoes in jackets until soft.
Cool and peel.
Dice potatoes, eggs, onion and celery.
Grate carrots.
To make dressing, mix together the dry ingredients, add eggs, vinegar and water.
Melt butter in saucepan and add dressing.
Cook until thickened.
Cool and pour over potato mixture and mix lightly.
If desired, ½ cup of sandwich spread or mayonnaise may be added to dressing before it is poured over vegetables.
Serves 8 to 10.

Turnip Slaw

6 medium-sized turnips	1 teaspoon salt
⅔ cup sour cream	2 tablespoons minced
2 tablespoons vinegar	parsley
2 tablespoons sugar	

Pare and grate raw turnips.
Pour over them a dressing made by combining the sugar, salt, vinegar and cream.
Garnish with parsley.
Serves 6.

Heavenly Salad

1 pound white grapes
One No. 2 can of pineapple (about 2¼ cups)
1 pound marshmallows, chopped
1 cup chopped nuts
2 cups whipping cream

Dressing:

3 egg yolks
½ teaspoon dry mustard
¼ teaspoon salt
Juice of 2 lemons

Split grapes in half lengthwise and remove seeds.
Add chopped pineapple and marshmallows.
Mix egg yolks, mustard, salt and lemon juice and cook until thickened. Cool.
Add whipped cream.
Pour dressing over fruit and mix lightly.
Let stand in the refrigerator overnight.
Add nuts just before serving.
Serve on lettuce or as a dessert.
Serves 8.

Chicken Salad

3 cups diced, cooked chicken
1½ cups diced celery
3 hard-cooked eggs
3 sweet pickles, chopped

1 teaspoon salt
⅛ teaspoon pepper
⅔ cup mayonnaise
3 tablespoons cream

Cut the cooked chicken in ½ inch pieces.
Chop celery and pickles and add to chicken.
Chop eggs, coarse, and add to mixture.
Add seasoning.
Add cream to mayonnaise; when smooth, mix with chicken.
Serve on lettuce.
Serves 8.

Cranberry Salad

½ pound cranberries
3 apples
1½ cups sugar
2 oranges or ½ cup crushed
   pineapple

¼ cup chopped walnuts
1 package cherry or
   strawberry gelatin
1 cup hot water
1 cup cold water

Wash and grind cranberries through food chopper.
Pare and core apples and chop very fine.
Add chopped oranges, nuts and sugar.
Dissolve gelatin in hot water.
Add cold water.
When cool, add salad mixture.
Pour into mold and allow to congeal.
Unmold on lettuce.
Serves 6.

Apple Salad

8 apples (Delicious
   preferred)
2 bananas
½ cup chopped celery
½ cup raisins

¼ cup coconut
½ cup peanuts
½ cup walnuts
Juice of ½ lemon
   (optional)

Dice apples, do not pare them.
Place them in weak salt water while other ingredients are
   prepared or add lemon juice and mix thoroughly. This
   keeps fruit from turning dark.
Drain and add chopped celery, bananas, raisins, coconut
   and nuts.

Make one of the two following salad dressings and pour over the apple mixture.
Serves 6-8.

Dressing:
I. Make a cooked dressing of the following:

1 cup water	1 tablespoon cornstarch
1 teaspoon vinegar	¼ cup cream
¼ teaspoon salt	1 teaspoon vanilla
1 cup sugar	

II. An uncooked dressing may be made as follows:

¼ cup peanut butter	½ cup sugar
¼ cup cream	½ cup mayonnaise

French Dressing

1 cup salad oil	1 teaspoon grated onion
1 cup vinegar	1 tablespoon Worcestershire
2 tablespoons sugar	sauce
1 teaspoon salt	1 cup catsup or condensed
1 teaspoon dry mustard	tomato soup

Mix sugar, salt, mustard and Worcestershire sauce together.
Add grated onion and catsup or tomato soup.
Add vinegar and pour on the oil slowly.
Place dressing in a bottle and keep in refrigerator.
Shake vigorously before using to blend ingredients.
Makes 1 pint dressing.

Cooked Salad Dressing

½ cup sugar
½ cup vinegar
½ cup water
1 egg or 2 yolks
1 tablespoon cornstarch or
  flour

1 teaspoon dry mustard
1 teaspoon salt
1 tablespoon butter

Mix sugar, salt, cornstarch and mustard.
Add egg and beat well.
Add water and vinegar.
Cook in the top of a double boiler until thickened.
Add butter and serve on potato salad, lettuce or cabbage.
Makes 1½ cups.

Fruit Salad Dressing

½ cup lemon or orange juice
½ cup pineapple juice
2 eggs
1½ tablespoons flour

½ cup sugar
1 cup whipping cream
½ cup walnuts (optional)

Combine juices and stir slowly into sugar and flour mixture.
Cook in a double boiler until it thickens.
Add beaten eggs and cook 1 minute longer; remove from
  heat and cool.
Fold in whipped cream.
Makes 2½ cups dressing.

Cakes
and
Frostings

Chapter VIII

Busy Day Cake

1⅜ cups all-purpose flour or 2 cups cake flour	⅓ cup shortening
1 cup sugar	1 egg
½ teaspoon salt	⅔ cup milk
2½ teaspoons baking powder	1 teaspoon vanilla

For ease in measuring: Pour milk into measuring cup up to ⅔ mark.

Add shortening, keeping it under the milk until it reaches the line indicating 1 cup.

Sift flour; measure and add sugar, salt, and baking powder. Sift again.

Add shortening, milk, unbeaten egg and vanilla all at once to sifted dry ingredients.

Beat well for 2½ minutes (electric mixer preferred).

If beating is done by hand, it is best to count the strokes. Try to average 130 strokes per minute. This should be done rather rapidly.

Pour into a greased oblong pan 8 x 12 inches.

Bake at 350° for 35 to 40 minutes.

While cake is baking, mix together the following:

3 tablespoons melted butter	⅔ cup brown sugar, packed
4 tablespoons cream	½ cup shredded coconut

Spread mixture on cake while it is warm.

Do not remove cake from pan.

Put cake under the broiler until frosting begins to bubble.

Applesauce Cake

½ cup shortening
1½ cups sugar
2 eggs, well beaten
1½ cups applesauce, unsweet-
ened
2½ cups cake flour
½ teaspoon salt
1 teaspoon soda dissolved
in 2 tablespoons hot wa-
ter

1 teaspoon cinnamon
½ teaspoon cloves
1 cup chopped seedless
raisins
½ cup chopped nuts (op-
tional)

Cream shortening. Add sugar gradually and continue to
beat until fluffy.

Add well-beaten eggs and combine thoroughly.

Sift flour; measure and sift again with salt and spices.

Add ⅓ of the applesauce to creamed mixture and blend.

Add dry ingredients alternately with remaining applesauce, beating thoroughly after each addition.

Dissolve soda in hot water and add to mixture. Mix
thoroughly.

Chop raisins and nuts on a board and flour lightly.

Fold these into mixture.

Pour into a large, greased loaf pan 5 x 9 x 4 inches.

Bake at 350° for approximately 1 hour.

Excellent flavor and keeps well.

For variation, replace half of the applesauce with ¾ cup
strained apricot pulp.

Fruit Cake (White)

¼ pound mixed lemon, orange and citron peel (candied)

1¼ pounds (4 cups) crystallized fruit—cherries, apricots, pineapple and plums

½ cup preserved ginger

¼ pound maraschino cherries

¼ pound blanched almonds

2½ cups cake flour

1 teaspoon baking powder

½ teaspoon salt

1 cup shortening

1 cup sugar

1 tablespoon lemon juice

8 egg whites

Cut peel and crystallized fruit in thin slices.

Blanch almonds by allowing to stand in boiling water for 5 minutes.

Slip off skins and dry.

Sift flour; measure and add baking powder and salt. Sift again.

Add 1 cup of this mixture to sliced peel, fruit and nuts. Stir well.

Cream shortening until light.

Add ½ cup sugar and remaining flour gradually and beat until fluffy.

Add floured fruits and nuts.

Mix well.

Add lemon juice to egg whites and beat until stiff.

Fold into beaten whites the remaining ½ cup of sugar.

Fold egg whites into cake mixture.

Bake in large tube pan or 2 loaf pans 5 x 9 x 4 inches lined with waxed paper.

Bake at 250° for approximately 3 hours.

Makes a cake weighing 3½ to 4 pounds.

This cake is very attractive if whole almonds and pieces of colored fruit are arranged so as to make a design on top of the cake.

Boiled Raisin Cake

1 pound seedless raisins	¼ teaspoon nutmeg
2 cups water	½ teaspoon cloves
⅔ cup shortening	1 teaspoon cinnamon
1½ cups sugar (half brown and half white sugar)	1 cup sour milk or butter-milk
3 cups all-purpose flour	1 cup chopped nuts
1 teaspoon salt	1 teaspoon vanilla
1½ teaspoons soda	

Chop raisins very fine and boil in the water until most of it is absorbed.

Add shortening to raisins and stir until it is melted.

Then add sugar and stir until it is entirely dissolved.

Sift flour; measure and sift again with salt, soda and spices.

Pour mixture into a bowl and add sifted dry ingredients alternately with milk.

Beat thoroughly after each addition.

Chop nuts and dust lightly with flour; add to mixture.

Pour into a large, greased loaf pan 5 x 9 x 4 inches.

Bake at 325° for 1 hour and 15 minutes.

A splendid fruit type of cake with fine keeping qualities.

Raw Apple Cake

½ cup shortening	1 teaspoon cinnamon
1 cup sugar	1½ cups ground raw apples (tart ones)
2 cups cake flour	1 cup chopped raisins
½ teaspoon salt	1 cup chopped nuts
1½ teaspoons soda	

Sift flour; measure and add sugar, soda, salt and cinnamon. Sift again.

Work the shortening into this mixture as for pastry.

Stir in chopped nuts and raisins that have been dusted with flour.

Add ground apples and stir only enough to blend ingredients together.

Pour into a greased loaf pan.

Tiptop Cake

½ cup shortening
1½ cups sugar
2 eggs
2¼ cups all-purpose flour

½ teaspoon salt
2 teaspoons baking powder
1 cup milk
1 teaspoon vanilla

Cream shortening and add sugar gradually.

Add beaten eggs and beat until light and fluffy.

Sift flour; measure and add salt and baking powder. Sift again.

Add dry ingredients alternately with milk and flavoring.

Beat thoroughly after each addition.

Pour into greased loaf or layer pans.

Makes 2 (8 inch) layers or 1 loaf 3½ x 8 x 4 inches.

Bake at 350° for 30 minutes for layers and 45 minutes for loaf.

An inexpensive cake that even a child can make with success.

Jelly Roll

3 eggs
1 cup sugar
3 tablespoons water or milk
1⅛ cups cake flour

½ teaspoon salt
1½ teaspoons baking powder
Grated rind of 1 lemon

Beat eggs until thick and lemon-colored.

Add sifted sugar gradually and continue beating.

Add liquid and lemon rind and beat.

Sift flour; measure and add salt and baking powder. Sift again.

Sift slowly over egg mixture, folding in with a wire whisk.

Cover a shallow-sided, flat pan 12 x 16 x ½ inches with waxed paper.

Pour dough into pan. (It should not be over ¼ inch thick in pan.)

Bake at 400° for 12 to 14 minutes.

Turn out on damp cloth that has been sprinkled with powdered sugar.

Remove waxed paper and trim off hard crusts.

Spread with tart jelly and roll immediately.

Delicious.

Old-time Pound Cake

1½ cups butter	½ teaspoon baking powder
2 cups sugar	½ teaspoon salt
2¾ cups all-purpose flour or 3 cups cake flour	1 teaspoon vanilla or lemon extract
8 eggs	

Cream butter.

Add sugar gradually and beat until fluffy.

Add eggs, 1 at a time, beating vigorously after each addition.

Sift flour; measure and sift again with salt and baking powder.

Add sifted dry ingredients alternately with eggs and flavoring.

Beat mixture until it is light enough to float when a little is dropped in water.

Pour into greased tube, loaf pan.

Bake at 350° for 1 hour.

This is a rich cake of golden-yellow color and a favorite of Grandmother's day.

Butter Frosting

3 tablespoons butter	1½ cups confectioner's sugar
1 tablespoon cream or strong coffee	½ teaspoon vanilla
	½ teaspoon almond extract

Cream butter until soft.
Add sugar, cream or coffee and flavoring.
Beat with electric or hand beater until smooth and creamy.
Spread on cake.

Caramel Frosting

3 cups brown sugar	2 tablespoons butter
1 cup top milk or thin cream	1 teaspoon vanilla

Mix ingredients together in a saucepan.
Stir until sugar is dissolved.
Cook syrup until it forms a soft ball when dropped in cold water (238°).
Cool until you can hold your hand on the bottom of the pan.
Beat until creamy and spread on cake.
Sprinkle with chopped nuts.

Chocolate Icing Deluxe

1 large egg	2 squares unsweetened chocolate
2 cups confectioner's sugar	
¼ teaspoon salt	1 teaspoon vanilla
⅓ cup butter or margarine	

Beat egg with electric or rotary beater until fluffy.
Sift the sugar and add gradually to the egg.
Add salt, soft shortening and melted chocolate.
Beat until smooth and creamy.
Add vanilla.
Spread on cake.

72

Cookies

Chapter IX

Chocolate Chip or Toll House Cookies

½ cup butter
½ cup brown sugar
½ cup granulated sugar
1 egg
1½ cups flour
½ teaspoon salt
½ teaspoon soda

1 packages chocolate bits (7 oz.)
1 tablespoon hot water
1 teaspoon vanilla
½ cup chopped nuts (optional)

Cream shortening and sugar together.
Add egg, water and vanilla and beat until fluffy.
Sift flour.
Measure and add salt and soda. Sift again.
Add sifted dry ingredients and beat until smooth.
Add chocolate bits and nuts and blend into mixture.
Drop by teaspoonfuls onto a greased baking sheet, spaced
    2 to 3 inches apart.
Bake at 375° for 10 minutes or until a light brown.
Makes about 4½ dozen cookies.

Christmas Fruit Cookies

½ cup shortening
½ cup butter
2 cups sugar
3 eggs
3¼ cups flour
½ teaspoon salt
1 teaspoon cinnamon
½ teaspoon each of nutmeg
    and cloves
¼ cup milk

1 teaspoon lemon extract
1½ teaspoons vanilla
½ pound dates, chopped
½ pound raisins, chopped
¼ pound candied cherries
¼ pound candied pineapple
¼ pound citron
1 pound English or black
    walnuts, chopped
1 teaspoon baking soda

Cream shortening and sugar together.
Add eggs and flavoring.
Beat until fluffy.
Sift flour.

Measure and add salt and spices.
Sift again.
Add sifted dry ingredients alternately with milk.
Mix thoroughly after each addition.
Dissolve soda in 1 tablespoon water and blend well into mixture.
Add chopped fruits and nuts and blend well into mixture.
Drop by teaspoonfuls onto greased baking sheet, spaced 2 to 3 inches apart.
Bake at 350° for about 15 minutes or until lightly browned.
Makes approximately 12 dozen cookies.

Peanut Butter Cookies

1 cup shortening	3 cups flour
1 cup peanut butter	½ teaspoon salt
1 cup brown sugar	2 teaspoons soda
1 cup granulated sugar	1 teaspoon baking powder
2 eggs	1 teaspoon vanilla

Cream shortening and peanut butter together.
Add sugar and continue to beat.
Add eggs and vanilla and beat until fluffy.
Sift flour.
Measure and add salt, soda and baking powder.
Sift again.
Gradually add sifted dry ingredients to creamed mixture and mix thoroughly.
Chill dough in refrigerator for several hours.
Shape dough into balls 1 inch in diameter.
Place balls 2 to 3 inches apart on greased baking sheet.
Press flat with a fork.
Bake at 375° for 12 to 15 minutes.
Makes about 7 dozen cookies.

Molasses Crinkles

¾ cup shortening	½ teaspoon salt
1 cup brown sugar	2 teaspoons soda
1 egg	1 teaspoon cinnamon
4 tablespoons molasses	1 teaspoon ginger
2¼ cups flour	½ teaspoon cloves

Cream shortening and sugar together.
Add egg and molasses and beat until well blended.
Sift flour.
Measure and add salt, soda and spices.
Sift again.
Add sifted dry ingredients to creamed mixture and mix thoroughly.
Chill dough in refrigerator.
Shape the chilled dough in balls 1 inch in diameter.
Roll balls in granulated sugar and place 2 inches apart on greased baking sheet.
Bake at 350° for 12 to 15 minutes.
Makes 4 dozen cookies.

Oatmeal Drop Cookies

1 cup shortening	2 cups rolled oats
1½ cups sugar	1 teaspoon cinnamon
2 eggs	½ cup sour milk
1¾ cups flour	1 cup chopped raisins or
½ teaspoon salt	dates
1 teaspoon baking powder	½ cup chopped nuts
1 teaspoon soda	

Cream shortening and sugar together.
Add eggs and beat until fluffy.
Sift flour.

Measure and add salt, soda, baking powder and cinnamon. Sift again.

Add rolled oats and mix thoroughly.

Add dry ingredients alternately with milk to creamed mixture.

Mix thoroughly.

Fold in chopped raisins or dates and nuts and stir until well blended.

Drop by teaspoonfuls onto greased baking sheet, spaced 2 to 3 inches apart.

Flatten with a fork.

Bake at 350° for 12 to 15 minutes.

Makes 6 dozen cookies.

Crunchy Crisps

1 cup shortening (half butter)	1¼ cups rolled oats
1½ cups brown sugar	¼ teaspoon salt
1 egg	2 teaspoons baking powder
1½ cups flour	1 cup grated coconut
	1 teaspoon vanilla

Cream shortening and sugar together.

Add vanilla.

Add egg and beat until fluffy.

Sift flour.

Measure and add salt and baking powder.

Sift again.

Add dry ingredients and rolled oats to creamed mixture. Mix thoroughly.

Add grated coconut and blend well into dough.

Drop by teaspoonfuls onto greased baking sheet, spaced 2 to 3 inches apart or roll in small balls and press flat with a fork.

Bake at 375° approximately 12 minutes.

Makes about 3 dozen cookies.

Old-Fashioned Ginger Cookies (Leb Kuchen)

2 cups shortening, melted	2 tablespoons soda
3 cups sorghum molasses	1 tablespoon ginger
1 cup sugar	1 tablespoon cinnamon
8 to 10 cups flour	1½ cups buttermilk or sour
1 teaspoon salt	milk

Heat molasses and sugar together.
When sugar is dissolved, add shortening and stir until it is
    melted.
Remove from heat. Cool to lukewarm.
Sift flour, salt, soda and spices together.
Add sifted dry ingredients alternately with sour milk.
Stir until a medium-soft dough is formed.
Work dough with hands for 5 minutes.
Let chill in refrigerator for several hours.
Turn dough onto lightly floured board and roll ¼ inch
    thick.
Cut with large round cookie or a doughnut cutter with
    center removed.
Glaze with a beaten egg. (Dip a small piece of cheesecloth
    in beaten egg and rub lightly over cookie.)
Place 1 inch apart on greased cookie sheet.
Bake at 350° for 20 to 25 minutes.
This is the soft, chewy cookie that was a favorite of grand-
    mother's day.
It is still very popular among many Mennonite families.
Makes 8 dozen large cookies.

Sand Tarts or Saint Hearts

1 cup shortening	1 teaspoon salt
2 cups granulated sugar	2 teaspoons baking powder
3 eggs	1 teaspoon vanilla or lemon
3½ to 4 cups flour	extract

Cream shortening and sugar together.

Add eggs and flavoring and beat until fluffy.
Sift flour.
Measure and add salt and baking powder.
Sift again.
Add sifted dry ingredients.
Stir until a medium-soft dough is formed.
Chill several hours in refrigerator.
Roll very thin and cut in fancy shapes.
Brush tops with rich milk and sprinkle with sugar and cinnamon.
Decorate with pecan halves.
Place 1 inch apart on a greased cookie sheet.
Bake at 350° for 8 to 10 minutes.
Makes 4 to 5 dozen cookies.
The oldest recipe books call these cookies Saint Hearts.

Sugar Cookies

1 cup shortening	1 teaspoon salt
2 cups sugar, granulated or light brown	1½ teaspoons baking powder
	1 teaspoon soda
2 eggs	¼ cup milk
Approximately 5 cups flour	1 teaspoon vanilla

Cream shortening and sugar together. Add flavoring.
Use half butter for good flavor.
Add eggs and beat until fluffy.
Sift flour.
Measure and add salt, soda and baking powder.
Sift again.
Add sifted dry ingredients alternately with milk.
Stir until dough is smooth.
Chill in refrigerator for several hours.
Roll out to ¼ inch thickness and cut in fancy shapes.
Place 1 inch apart on greased cookie sheet and bake at 400° for 8 to 10 minutes.
Makes about 6 dozen cookies.

Raisin Filled Cookies

1 cup shortening	4 teaspoons baking powder
2 cups sugar	1 teaspoon soda
2 eggs	1 cup milk
Approximately 5½ cups flour	2 teaspoons vanilla
1 teaspoon salt	

Cream shortening and sugar together. Add vanilla.
Add eggs and beat until fluffy.
Sift flour.
Measure and add salt, soda and baking powder.
Sift again.
Add sifted dry ingredients alternately with milk.
Stir until smooth.
Add more flour if necessary.
Chill dough for several hours in refrigerator.
Turn out on lightly floured board and roll to ⅛ inch thickness.
Cut with round cutter and place 1 inch apart on a greased cookie sheet.
Spread with the following filling:

2 cups ground raisins	2 tablespoons flour
1 cup sugar	½ cup chopped nuts
1 cup water	

Combine ingredients and cook until thick, stirring constantly.
Cool before spreading on cookie.
Put a teaspoon of filling in center of each and cover with another round of dough.
Press edges together.
Bake at 400° for 10 to 12 minutes.
Makes 4 dozen cookies.

Peppernuts (Pfeffernusse)

⅓ cup shortening
1 cup sugar
Approximately 6 cups flour
3 teaspoons baking powder
½ teaspoon salt

1 cup sweet cream
1 cup milk
1 teaspoon peppermint
   extract

Cream shortening and sugar together.
Add flavoring.
Add sweet cream and beat until fluffy.
Sift flour.
Measure and add baking powder and salt.
Sift again.
Add sifted dry ingredients alternately with milk.
Beat until a medium-soft, smooth dough is formed.
Chill dough in refrigerator for several hours.
When thoroughly chilled, divide dough into 5 or 6 parts.
Remove one portion from refrigerator at a time and turn out on lightly floured board.
Cut off small portions and form into fingerlike sticks, rolling with the flat part of hand.
Lay sticks in parallel rows and cut across, making pieces the size of a small marble.
Place pieces close together on a greased baking sheet.
Bake at 425° until they begin to turn a light, golden brown.
These cookies are especially popular at Christmas time in many Mennonite homes.

Butterscotch Squares

¼ cup butter
1 cup brown sugar
1 egg
1 cup flour

1 teaspoon baking powder
¼ teaspoon salt
½ cup chopped nuts
1 teaspoon vanilla

Melt butter and blend with sugar.
Add egg and beat vigorously.
Sift flour.
Measure and add baking powder and salt.
Sift again.
Add dry ingredients to egg and sugar mixture and mix together well.
Add chopped nuts and vanilla.
Spread dough in a greased pan 8 x 8 inches.
Bake at 350° for 30 minutes.
Cut in squares or bars while warm.
Makes 18 to 20 squares.

Date Bars

⅔ cup shortening
1 cup brown sugar
2 eggs
1 cup flour

1 teaspoon baking powder
½ teaspoon salt
1 cup chopped dates
1 cup chopped nuts

Cream shortening and sugar together.
Add eggs to creamed mixture, and beat until light and fluffy.
Sift flour.
Measure and add baking powder and salt.
Sift again.
Add sifted dry ingredients to mixture.
Fold in chopped dates and nuts.
Turn into a greased baking pan 8 x 10 inches.
Bake at 350° for about 25 minutes.
Cut in bars while still warm and roll in powdered sugar.
Makes 2 dozen bars.

Desserts

Chapter X

Baked Cup Custards

4 eggs
½ cup sugar
½ teaspoon salt

4 cups milk
½ teaspoon vanilla
Nutmeg (optional)

Beat eggs slightly.
Add sugar, salt and vanilla.
Scald milk and pour it slowly over egg mixture.
Stir until thoroughly mixed.
Pour into custard cups, filling them two-thirds full.
Sprinkle with nutmeg if desired.
Set cups in a pan and pour hot water around them until it
    comes to the level of the custard.
Bake at 325° approximately 40 minutes, or until a silver
    knife comes out clean when inserted in the center of the
    custard.
Custard may also be baked in a casserole.
Serve with whipped cream if desired.
Makes 8 custards.

Coconut Cream Tapioca

1 quart milk (4 cups)
1 cup sugar
4 eggs, separated

3 tablespoons minute tapioca
¼ teaspoon salt
½ cup shredded coconut

Scald milk in top of double boiler.
Add salt and minute tapioca and cook 15 minutes or until
    clear.
Stir frequently.
Combine egg yolks, sugar and coconut.
Add some of the hot mixture and stir until a smooth paste
    is formed.

Add paste to hot tapioca and continue to cook for 2 minutes, stirring constantly.

Pour into a greased baking dish.

Cover with a meringue made by adding 4 tablespoons sugar to stiffly beaten egg whites.

Sprinkle with coconut.

Bake at 300° for 15 minutes or until a golden brown.

Makes 6-8 servings.

Creamy Rice Pudding

¼ cup uncooked rice	6 tablespoons sugar
2 cups milk	¼ teaspoon salt
2 eggs, separated	1 teaspoon vanilla

Wash rice, drain and add to milk.

Cook covered in top of double boiler until rice is tender (about 45 minutes).

Beat egg yolks thoroughly. Add 4 tablespoons sugar and salt.

Stir some of the rice mixture into beaten yolks.

Then add yolks to hot mixture and cook 2 minutes.

Stir constantly.

Remove from heat and add vanilla.

Beat egg whites until stiff, add 2 tablespoons sugar.

Fold beaten whites into custard.

Chill and serve.

Beaten whites may be spread on top of custard and browned delicately in the oven.

One cup of raisins may be cooked in custard if desired.

Makes 6 servings.

Floating Island Custard

1 quart milk (4 cups)	2 tablespoons cornstarch
2 eggs, separated	¼ teaspoon salt
½ cup sugar	1 teaspoon vanilla

Scald 3½ cups milk in top of double boiler.

Combine sugar, salt and cornstarch.

Add remaining milk to make a smooth paste.

Slowly add paste to hot milk and cook until thickened.

Stir constantly.

Beat egg yolks, add some of the hot custard.

Then add egg yolks to custard and cook 2 minutes longer.

Remove custard from heat and add vanilla. Chill.

Beat egg whites until stiff, add 4 tablespoons of sugar and
½ teaspoon vanilla.

Drop meringue by spoonfuls onto chilled custard.

Top with red jelly.

Makes 6-8 servings.

Cracker Pudding

4 cups milk	1 cup shredded coconut
2 eggs, separated	1 teaspoon vanilla
½ cup sugar	
2 cups coarse cracker crumbs	

Scald milk in top of double boiler.

Beat egg yolks and add sugar.

Add this mixture gradually to scalded milk. Stir constantly.

Allow to cook for one minute and then add cracker
crumbs and coconut.

Stir until cracker crumbs are soft and mixture is thick.

Remove from heat and add vanilla.

Pour into a buttered baking dish.

Spread with meringue made by beating 3 tablespoons sugar into stiffly beaten egg whites.
Bake at 350° until meringue is a golden brown.
Makes 6-8 servings.

Old-fashioned Apple Dumplings

6 medium-sized baking ap-
ples
2 cups flour
2½ teaspoons baking powder

½ teaspoon salt
⅔ cup shortening
½ cup milk

Pare and core apples. Leave whole.
To make pastry, sift flour, baking powder and salt together.
Cut in shortening until particles are about the size of small peas.
Sprinkle milk over mixture and press together lightly, working dough only enough to hold together.
Roll dough as for pastry and cut into 6 squares and place an apple on each.
Fill cavity in apple with sugar and cinnamon.
Pat dough around apple to cover it completely.
Fasten edges securely on top of apple.
Place dumplings 1 inch apart in a greased baking pan.
Pour over them the sauce made as follows:

Sauce:
2 cups brown sugar
2 cups water
¼ cup butter

¼ teaspoon cinnamon or
nutmeg (optional)

Combine brown sugar, water and spices.
Cook for 5 minutes, remove from heat and add butter.
Bake at 375° for 35 to 40 minutes.
Baste occasionally during baking.
Serve hot with rich milk or cream.

Apple Fritters

1 cup flour	1 egg, beaten
1½ teaspoons baking powder	½ cup milk plus
½ teaspoon salt	1 tablespoon
2 tablespoons sugar	1½ cups apples, chopped

Sift dry ingredients together.
Beat egg and add milk.
Pour into dry ingredients.
Stir until the batter is smooth.
Pare apples and dice or slice very thin.
Add apples to batter and blend together.
Drop by spoonfuls into deep hot fat 370° to 375°.
Fry until a golden brown on all sides.
Makes 12 to 15 fritters.

Apple Goodie

¾ cup sugar	For topping:
1 tablespoon flour	½ cup oatmeal
⅛ teaspoon salt	½ cup brown sugar
½ teaspoon cinnamon	½ cup flour
2 cups sliced apples	¼ cup butter
	⅛ teaspoon soda
	⅛ teaspoon baking powder

Sift sugar, flour, salt, cinnamon together and combine with
  sliced apples.
Mix together well and place in the bottom of a greased
  casserole.
To make topping, combine dry ingredients and rub in but-
  ter to make crumbs.
Put crumbs on top of apple mixture.
Bake at 375° for 35 to 40 minutes.
Serve hot or cold with rich milk.
Makes 6 servings.

Pluma Moos

2 quarts water	½ cup sugar
1 cup seedless raisins	6 tablespoons flour
1 cup dried prunes	½ teaspoon salt
¼ cup dried peaches	1 teaspoon cinnamon
¼ cup dried apricots	1 cup sweet or sour cream

Wash fruit and add warm water.

Cook until almost tender and then add sugar.

While fruit is cooking, prepare flour paste by combining flour, salt, cinnamon and cream.

When fruit is done, slowly add flour paste, stirring constantly.

Cook until slightly thickened.

Serve warm.

This dish is served traditionally as a dessert or side dish in some Mennonite communities for Easter, Pentecost or Christmas dinners.

Makes 8 servings.

Berry Sturm

1 quart berries (raspberry, blackberry or blueberry)	¾ cup sugar
	12 slices bread (a day old)
	1 pint rich milk

Mash fruit and add sugar.

Cut bread into small cubes and add to berries.

Let stand 10 minutes and then add cold milk.

This dish is of Swiss origin.

Makes 6 servings.

Prune Whip

2 cups prune pulp
3 egg whites
½ cup sugar

¼ teaspoon salt
2 tablespoons lemon juice

Beat egg whites with salt until stiff but not dry.
Add sugar gradually, beating into whites.
Add lemon juice to prune pulp and gradually beat into egg
    whites.
Continue to beat until mixture is fluffy.
Pile lightly into individual serving dishes and chill.
Or pour into a greased baking dish, set in a pan of water
    and bake at 300° for 25 minutes.
Serve with whipped cream or a custard sauce.
Makes 6 servings.

Rhubarb Crunch

Mix until crumbly:
  1 cup flour, sifted
  ¾ cup uncooked oatmeal
  1 cup brown sugar, packed
  ½ cup melted butter
  1 teaspoon cinnamon
Prepare 4 cups diced rhubarb

Combine the following:
  1 cup sugar
  2 tablespoons cornstarch
  1 cup water
  1 teaspoon vanilla

Press half of crumbs in a greased 9 inch baking pan.
Add diced rhubarb.
Combine second mixture and cook until thick and clear.
Pour over rhubarb.
Top with remaining crumbs.
Bake at 350° for 35 to 40 minutes.
Cut in squares and serve while warm.
This is delicious served plain or with cream.
Makes 8 servings.

Buttermilk Pineapple Sherbet

1 cup crushed pineapple
¾ cup sugar
Juice of 1 lemon

2 cups buttermilk
1 egg white

Combine sugar and crushed pineapple.
Add lemon juice and buttermilk.
Freeze until firm and then remove from tray and break up
  with a wooden spoon.
Beat with electric mixer or rotary beater until smooth.
Add stiffly beaten egg white and blend into mixture.
Return to refrigerator to finish freezing.
Makes 6-8 servings.

Graham Cracker Fluff

2 egg yolks
½ cup sugar
⅔ cup milk
1 package gelatin (1 tablespoon)
½ cup cold water

2 egg whites
1 cup whipping cream
1 teaspoon vanilla
3 tablespoons melted butter
3 tablespoons sugar
12 graham crackers

Beat egg yolks and add sugar and milk.
Cook in top of double boiler until slightly thickened.
Soak gelatin in the cold water.
Pour hot mixture over softened gelatin and stir until
  smooth.
Chill until slightly thickened.
Add stiffly beaten egg whites, vanilla and whipped cream
  to chilled mixture.
Combine melted butter, cracker crumbs and sugar to
  make crumbs.
Sprinkle half of crumbs in bottom of serving dish.
Add mixture and top with remaining crumbs.
Let chill in refrigerator until set.
Makes 6-8 servings.

Peach Marlow

32 marshmallows	1 cup crushed peaches
2 tablespoons water	(fresh or canned)
1 tablespoon lemon juice	1 cup whipping cream

Chop marshmallows and add water.

Heat in a saucepan over low heat, folding over and over until marshmallows are almost melted.

Remove from heat and continue folding until mixture is smooth.

Cool and then fold in crushed peaches.

Add lemon juice and whipped cream.

Pour mixture in freezing tray and freeze until set but not hard.

Makes 6-8 servings.

Apricot Upside Down Cake

18 apricot halves	5 tablespoons apricot juice
½ cup shortening	1 cup cake flour
1 cup brown sugar	1 teaspoon baking powder
3 eggs, separated	¼ teaspoon salt
1 cup granulated sugar	

Melt butter in large frying pan.

Add brown sugar.

Arrange apricot halves on top of sugar-butter mixture.

Beat egg yolks until light.

Add granulated sugar and apricot juice.

Sift flour and measure.

Sift flour, salt and baking powder together.

Add to mixture.

Fold in stiffly beaten egg whites.

Pour mixture over apricots and bake at 375° for 35 to 40 minutes.

Serve upside down.

Garnish with whipped cream.

Makes 6-8 servings.

Pastry, Pies and Tarts

Chapter XI

Pastry (for a 9-inch double-crust pie)

2¼ cups flour   ½ teaspoon salt
⅔ cup shortening   ⅓ cup cold water

Combine flour and salt in a mixing bowl.

Cut shortening into flour with a pastry blender or two knives.

Do not overmix; these are sufficiently blended when particles are the size of peas.

Add water gradually, sprinkling 1 tablespoon at a time over mixture.

Toss lightly with a fork until all particles of flour have been dampened.

Use only enough water to hold the pastry together when it is pressed between the fingers. It should not feel wet.

Roll dough into a round ball, handling as little as possible.

Roll out on a lightly floured board into a circle ⅛ inch thick and 1 inch larger than the diameter of the top of the pan.

Coconut Cream Pie

2 cups milk   ½ teaspoon salt
½ cup sugar   1¼ cups shredded coconut
4 tablespoons cornstarch   1 teaspoon vanilla
2 eggs, separated   Pastry for 1 (9 inch) crust
1 tablespoon butter   (page 94)

Scald 1½ cups milk in top of double boiler.

Combine sugar, salt and cornstarch.

Add remaining milk.

Pour paste into hot milk and cook until thickened.

Beat egg yolks.

Pour small amount of hot mixture over yolks before adding them to milk.

Cook 2 minutes longer.

Remove from heat, add butter, vanilla and ¾ cup shredded coconut.

Cool and pour into baked shell.

Cover with meringue made by adding 4 tablespoons sugar to beaten egg white.

Sprinkle remaining coconut over top and bake at 350° until golden brown.

Makes 1 (9 inch) pie.

Funny Cake Pie

Top Part:
- ½ cup sugar
- ¼ cup shortening
- 1 egg
- ½ cup milk
- 1 teaspoon baking powder
- 1 cup flour
- ½ teaspoon vanilla

Lower Part:
- ½ cup sugar
- ¼ cup cocoa
- ⅓ cup hot water
- ¼ teaspoon vanilla
- Pastry for 1 (9 inch) crust (page 94)

Mix top part like cake batter, creaming fat, and adding sugar and egg.

Add milk alternately with sifted dry ingredients.

For lower part, combine sugar and cocoa.

Add hot water and vanilla.

Line pie plate with pastry.

Add lower part first and then pour top part over it.

Bake at 375° for approximately 40 minutes.

Makes 1 (9 inch) pie.

Apple Pie

3 cups diced apples
⅔ cup sugar
1 tablespoon flour
½ teaspoon cinnamon or
  nutmeg

2 tablespoons rich milk
2 tablespoons butter
  (optional)
Pastry for two 9 inch crusts
  (page 94)

Mix apples, sugar, flour and spice together until well
  blended.
Place mixture in unbaked crust.
Add rich milk and dots of butter over the top.
Place strips or top crust on pie as desired.
Fasten securely at edges.
Bake in hot oven, 400° for 50 minutes.
Makes 1 (9 inch) pie.

Dried Snitz Pie

2 cups dried tart apples
⅔ cup sugar
1½ cups water
¼ teaspoon powdered cloves

½ teaspoon cinnamon
Pastry for 2 (9 inch) crusts
  (page 94)

Soak apples in 1½ cups warm water.
Cook apples in water in which they were soaked.
When soft, rub apples through a colander.
Add sugar and spices.
Put mixture in an unbaked pie shell.
Cover pie with top crust. Fasten at edges.
Bake at 425° for 15 minutes, reduce temperature to 375°
  and continue to bake for 35 minutes.
This makes 1 (9 inch) pie.

Cherry Pie

2½ cups sour cherries
⅓ cup cherry juice
⅓ cup brown sugar
⅓ cup granulated sugar
3 tablespoons minute tapioca

1 tablespoon butter
⅛ teaspoon almond extract
Pastry for 2 (9 inch) crusts (page 94)

Combine cherries, juice, sugars, flavoring and tapioca.
Let stand 15 minutes.
Pour into pastry-lined pie plate. Dot with butter.
Place crust or strips on top as preferred.
Bake at 425° for 10 minutes, then in moderate oven (375°) for 30 minutes.
Makes 1 (9 inch) pie.

Green Tomato Pie

3 cups green tomatoes, sliced
½ cup brown sugar
½ cup molasses
½ cup water
2 tablespoons flour

1 teaspoon cinnamon
¼ teaspoon nutmeg
Pastry for 2 (9 inch) crusts (page 94)

Slice tomatoes in thin rings. Do not pare.
Cover with boiling water and let stand 10 minutes. Drain.
Put tomato slices in unbaked pastry shell.
Combine sugar, flour and spices.
Add molasses and water.
Pour mixture over tomatoes.
Cover with a top crust.
Bake at 425° for 15 minutes, reduce temperature to 375° and continue to bake 30 minutes.
Makes 1 (9 inch) pie.

Lemon Sponge

Juice and rind of 1 lemon
1 cup sugar
3 tablespoons flour
3 eggs, separated
½ teaspoon salt

2 tablespoons butter
1½ cups hot water or milk
Pastry for 1 (9 inch) crust
(page 94)

Cream butter, add sugar and egg yolks. Beat well. Add milk.
Add flour, salt, lemon juice, grated rind and water or milk.
Fold in stiffly beaten egg whites.
Pour in unbaked pie shell.
Bake at 350° for 40-45 minutes.
Makes 1 (9 inch) pie.

Raisin Pie

1 cup raisins
2 cups water
½ cup sugar
1 egg
3½ tablespoons flour or minute tapioca
¼ teaspoon salt

1 tablespoon butter
2 tablespoons lemon juice
1 teaspoon grated lemon rind
Pastry for 1 (9 inch) crust
(page 94)

Add warm water to raisins, cover and cook slowly for 20 minutes.
Drain and add enough water to juice to make 2 cups.
Combine flour or tapioca, sugar, salt and liquid.
Cook over direct heat until thickened, stirring constantly.
Pour small amount of hot mixture over beaten egg. Stir vigorously.
Return to saucepan and bring to a boil.
Remove from heat, add butter, lemon juice and rind.
Cool and pour into a baked shell.
Cover with whipped cream when serving.

For variety add 2 eggs. Separate eggs and use whites for meringue on top. Bake at 325° until a golden brown.

Old-Fashioned Baked Custard Pie

3 cups milk
3 eggs
⅓ cup sugar
½ teaspoon salt

2 teaspoons flour
¼ teaspoon nutmeg
Pastry for 1 (9 inch) crust
(page 94)

Combine sugar and flour.
Add beaten eggs.
Bring milk to boiling point and add gradually to egg mixture.
Pour into an unbaked pie shell and sprinkle nutmeg over the top.
Bake at 350° for 40-45 minutes or until an inserted silver knife comes out clean.
Makes 1 (9 inch) pie.

Pumpkin Pie

1½ cups cooked pumpkin
1 cup brown sugar
1½ cups milk, scalded
3 egg yolks
½ teaspoon salt
1 tablespoon cornstarch

¼ teaspoon ginger
¼ teaspoon cloves
1 teaspoon cinnamon
Pastry for 1 (9 inch) crust
(page 94)

Cook pumpkin and rub through a sieve.
Add beaten egg yolks, sugar, salt, cornstarch and spices.
Gradually add scalded milk and mix thoroughly.
Pour mixture into an unbaked crust.
Bake at 425° for 10 minutes, then reduce heat to 375° and continue baking for 30 minutes.
Makes 1 (9 inch) pie.

Rhubarb Pie

3 cups diced, pink rhubarb
1½ cups sugar
3 tablespoons flour
¼ teaspoon salt
1 tablespoon lemon
  or orange juice

2 eggs, separated
Pastry for 1 (9 inch) crust
  (page 94)

Cut rhubarb in pieces ¼ inch thick.
Arrange in an unbaked pie shell.
Combine sugar and flour, add egg yolks and lemon juice.
Stir until a smooth paste is formed.
Pour mixture over rhubarb.
Cover with meringue made with egg whites or with a top
  crust.
Bake at 425° for 10 minutes and then reduce heat to
  325° and bake for 30 more minutes.

Shoo Fly Pie

Bottom Part:
1 cup dark mild molasses
¾ cup boiling water
½ teaspoon soda

Top Part:
1½ cups flour
¼ cup shortening
½ cup brown sugar
Pastry for 1 (9 inch) crust
  (page 94)

Dissolve soda in hot water and add molasses.
Combine sugar and flour and rub in shortening to make
  crumbs.
Pour one-third of the liquid into an unbaked crust.
Add one-third of the crumb mixture.
Continue alternate layers, putting crumbs on top.
Bake at 375° for approximately 35 minutes.
Makes 1 (9 inch) pie.

Beverages

Chapter XII

Fruit Punch (With Tea Base)

1½ cups sugar	1½ cups lemon juice
1 cup water	2 cups orange juice
⅛ teaspoon salt	1 quart ginger ale
1½ cups strong tea infusion	Mint leaves

Combine sugar and water and cook on low heat for 1 minute.

Cool the syrup and pour over ice.

To make tea infusion, add 3 teaspoons tea to 1½ cups water.

Add the fruit juices, tea and salt and mix well.

Add ginger ale just before serving.

Place a sprig of mint in each glass as it is served.

Serves 12.

Spiced Punch

1½ cups sugar	1 quart orange juice (canned or fresh)
2 cups water	
1 teaspoon whole cloves	2 cups lemon juice
1 stick cinnamon (4 inches)	2 cups grapefruit juice
	2 cups pineapple juice

Simmer sugar, water and spices together for 10 minutes.

Strain and cool.

Add fruit juices.

Add ice when serving.

Serves 12.

Grape Juice

1 cup grapes	Boiling water
½ cup sugar	

Wash grapes and put them in a sterile quart jar.

Add sugar and fill jar with boiling water.

Stir with a silver spoon to dissolve sugar. Seal.
If silver spoon is placed in jar before boiling water is added, it will keep jar from cracking.

Lemonade

6 lemons	2½ quarts water
1½ cups sugar	

Slice lemons in thin rings and place in porcelain or enamel container.
Add sugar and pound with a wooden mallet to extract juice.
Let stand 20 minutes and then add cold water and ice cubes.
Stir until well blended.
Makes 3 quarts.
To use rind along with pulp and juice adds flavor and is also an economy.

Spiced Cider

6 cups sweet cider	½ teaspoon grated orange rind
20 whole cloves	
3 sticks cinnamon	
½ teaspoon grated lemon rind	

Combine spices and 3 cups cider and place over low heat.
Bring to boiling point and simmer 5 minutes.
Remove from heat and let stand 30 minutes.
Add remaining cider, orange and lemon rind. Chill.
When ready to serve, pour over ice cubes.
Garnish with orange or lemon slices.
Makes 8-10 servings.

Hot Chocolate

2 squares unsweetened chocolate (2 ounces)	⅛ teaspoon salt
	1 quart milk
⅓ cup sugar	½ cup boiling water

Grate chocolate in top of double boiler.
Add sugar, salt and boiling water and stir until a smooth paste.
Place pan over direct heat and cook syrup 3 minutes.
Add milk gradually and heat to boiling point.
Beat until frothy.
Add whipped cream or marshmallow to each cup.
Makes 6 servings.
If chocolate syrup is used, add 2 tablespoons for each cup of milk used.

Cocoa

3 tablespoons cocoa	⅛ teaspoon salt
⅓ cup sugar	6 marshmallows
½ cup warm water	½ teaspoon vanilla
1 quart milk	(optional)

Mix sugar, salt and cocoa together.
Add warm water and stir to a smooth paste.
Cook for 3 minutes.
Scald milk in top of double boiler.
Add slowly to cocoa mixture and stir until well blended.
Add vanilla.
Beat with a rotary egg beater until frothy.
Top each cup with a marshmallow or whipped cream.
Makes 6 servings.

Pickles
and
Relishes

Chapter XIII

Bread and Butter Pickle

30 medium-sized cucumbers, (1 gallon, sliced)
8 medium-sized onions
2 large red or green peppers
½ cup salt

5 cups sugar
5 cups vinegar
2 tablespoons mustard seed
1 teaspoon turmeric
1 teaspoon whole cloves

Slice cucumbers in thin rings. Do not pare.
Slice onions in thin rings.
Cut peppers in fine strips.
Dissolve salt in ice water and pour over sliced vegetables.
Let stand 3 hours and drain.
Combine vinegar, sugar and spices and bring to a boil.
Add drained vegetables and heat to boiling point. Do not boil.
Pack into sterilized jars and seal.

Dutch Lunch Pickles

1 gallon cucumbers, quartered lengthwise
4 cloves garlic
4 small onions
4 pieces dill or 4 grape leaves

4 cups vinegar
1 cup water
¼ cup salt
2 cups sugar
1 tablespoon mixed spices

Cut medium-sized cucumbers into quarters lengthwise.
Place in cold salt water overnight.
In the morning, drain and pack in jars.
Add 1 clove garlic, 1 sliced onion and 1 piece of dill or a grape leaf to each jar.
Combine vinegar, water, sugar and spices and bring to a boil.
Pour over pickles and seal or keep in refrigerator or cellar in a stone jar.
These are ready to eat in 1 week.

Granddaddy's Green Tomato Pickle

1 gallon green tomatoes, sliced	2 pints vinegar
10 medium-sized onions	¼ cup salt
1 tablespoon mustard seed	1 cup sugar

Slice tomatoes in thin slices, do not peel.

Slice onions in thin rings.

Place alternate layers of sliced tomato and onion in a crock.

Sprinkle with mustard seed and salt. Let stand overnight. Drain. Salt should not be added to vinegar.

Combine sugar and vinegar and pour over tomatoes.

Cover with a plate and let stand 24 hours before using.

This is a cold, crisp pickle. Very tasty.

Pickled Watermelon Rind

5 pounds watermelon rind	2 cups water
2½ pounds sugar	½ teaspoon oil of cloves
2 cups vinegar	½ teaspoon oil of cinnamon

Pare the watermelon and cut rind in 2 inch pieces.

Mix ½ cup salt with 2 quarts water and soak rind overnight.

Drain and rinse with clear water. Drain again.

Cook in fresh water until tender. Drain.

Combine sugar, vinegar, water and spices.

Bring the syrup to a boil and pour it over the rind.

Let stand overnight.

In the morning, drain off the syrup and cook it several minutes.

Repeat for 3 days.

On the third day, cook rind and syrup together for 3 minutes.

The fruit remains clear if the oil of spices are used.

Makes 6 pints.

Seven-Day Sweet Pickles

7 pounds medium-sized cucumbers
Water to cover
1 quart vinegar

8 cups sugar
2 tablespoons salt
2 tablespoons mixed pickle spices

Wash cucumbers and cover them with boiling water.
Let stand 24 hours and drain.
Repeat each day for 4 days, using fresh water each time.
On the fifth day, cut cucumbers in ¼ inch rings.
Combine vinegar, sugar, salt and spices.
Bring liquid to a boil and pour over sliced cucumbers.
Let stand 24 hours.
Drain syrup and bring to a boil.
Pour over cucumbers.
Repeat on the sixth day.
On the last day, drain off the syrup again and bring it to a boil.
Add cucumber slices and bring to the boiling point.
Pack into hot jars and seal.
These are very crisp and delicious pickles.

Catsup (Tomato)

½ bushel ripe tomatoes
2 large onions
6 peppers, red or green
1 bunch celery, chopped
4 sticks cinnamon bark
1 tablespoon whole cloves

2 tablespoons salt
2 teaspoons celery seed
2 teaspoons ground mustard
1 teaspoon paprika
2 cups sugar
3 cups vinegar

Cut the tomatoes into quarters. Do not peel.
Crush only enough to remove a small portion of juice.
Bring to a boil and cook for 3 minutes.
Pour through a sieve and let drain without crushing.
Cook onions, celery and peppers until tender and press through a sieve.

Mix tomato pulp with other strained vegetables.
Combine sugar, salt and vinegar.
Tie spices in a bag and add to liquid.
Boil liquid for 5 minutes, add vegetable pulp and simmer for 30 minutes.
Pour into hot jars and seal.
Makes approximately 14 quarts.

Chow Chow

1 quart cucumbers, diced	1 pint red peppers
1 quart string beans	1 cup small onions
1 quart Lima beans	1 tablespoon dry mustard
1 quart corn	2 cups sugar
1 pint celery	1 quart vinegar
1 pint green peppers	

Chop vegetables the desired size and cook separately.
Cook until tender, not soft.
Drain cooked vegetables and mix together.
Combine sugar, mustard and vinegar.
Bring to a boil.
Add mixed vegetables to hot liquid and bring to boiling point.
Put into hot jars and seal.

Beet Pickle (Cold)

1 gallon beets, cooked	2½ cups brown sugar
⅓ cup prepared mustard	3 cups vinegar
⅓ cup salt	½ cup cold water

Cook beets until tender. Skin.
Slice and place in a stone crock or jar.
Mix mustard, sugar and salt and add vinegar and water.
Pour mixture over beets and keep in a cool place.
These are ready to use after 24 hours.

End of the Garden Pickle

2 cups sliced cucumbers
2 cups chopped red or green peppers
2 cups chopped cabbage
2 cups chopped green tomatoes
2 cups green string beans
2 cups diced carrots

2 cups chopped celery
1 cup diced onion
2 tablespoons celery seed
4 tablespoons mustard seed
4 cups vinegar
4 cups sugar
2 tablespoons turmeric

Slice cucumbers. Chop cabbage, tomatoes and peppers.
Soak overnight in salt water, using ½ cup salt to 2 quarts water.
In the morning, cut string beans and chop carrots and celery.
Cook until tender, but not soft.
Drain vegetables which soaked overnight and combine with cooked vegetables.
Combine vinegar, sugar and spices and bring to a boil.
Add vegetables and simmer together for 10 minutes.
Pack into jars and seal.

Green String Bean Pickle

3 quarts string beans
2 tablespoons salt
3 cups sugar
3 pints vinegar

1 teaspoon ground mustard
1 teaspoon celery seed
2 teaspoons turmeric
¼ cup flour

Cut beans into 1 inch pieces.
Cook in salt water until tender, but not soft.
Combine sugar, salt, flour and spices with the vinegar.
Cook together until slightly thickened.
Add beans and bring to a boil.
Put into hot jars and seal.

Jellies,
Jams, Preserves

Chapter XIV

Apple Butter (Small Amount)

2 quarts apple cider	1 teaspoon powdered
4 quarts apples	cinnamon or ¼ teaspoon
2 cups sugar	oil of cinnamon
2 cups dark corn syrup	

Boil the cider until it is reduced to 1 quart.

Pare apples, core and slice in thin pieces.

Add apples to cider and cook slowly until the mixture begins to thicken.

Stir frequently.

Then add sugar, syrup and cinnamon.

Continue to cook until a little of the butter, when cooled on a plate, is of a good consistency to spread.

Yield 5 to 6 pints.

Apricot Jam

1 pound dried apricots	1 No. 2 can crushed
1 quart water	pineapple or 2 oranges
6 cups sugar	and 1 lemon

Soak apricots 3 hours in warm water.

Grind through medium-fine blade of food chopper.

If oranges are used, grind one orange with rind.

To the apricot pulp add pineapple or orange and lemon juice.

Add sugar and cook rapidly until thick.

Stir frequently.

Pour into jars and seal.

Cherry Preserves

3 pounds red cherries	3 pounds sugar

Stem and seed cherries.

Bring to boiling point, stirring frequently.

Add sugar gradually, stirring to keep from sticking.
Cook preserves 20 minutes.
Add a few drops of red coloring.
If they are not as thick as desired, drain liquid and cook to
    desired thickness.
Combine cherries and thickened syrup.
Pour into a crock or bowl and let stand 12 hours.
Put into jars and cover with paraffin.

Elderberry Jelly

2 cups elderberry juice   3 cups sugar
2 cups apple juice (thick)

Cook elderberries until soft and then strain.
Cook apples, which have not been pared, in a moderate
    amount of water.
When tender, strain through bag; do not squeeze.
Combine the juices and bring to a boil.
Add sugar gradually and cook rapidly.
Cook until the jelly stage has been reached.
Pour into hot jars and cover with paraffin.

Grape Conserve

6 pounds grapes (stemmed)   3 oranges
6 pounds sugar   1 cup chopped nuts
1 pound raisins

Remove hulls and cook pulp until tender.
Rub through a sieve to remove seeds.
Combine pulp and hulls.
Add sugar, raisins, juice and grated rind of oranges.
Cook until thick.
Add nuts and remove from heat.
Pour into hot glasses and seal with paraffin.

Crab Apple Jelly

4 cups crab apple juice   3 cups sugar

Wash apples and cut into quarters.
Do not pare.
Put apples in a saucepan.
Add enough water until it can be seen through pieces of fruit.
Cover and cook slowly until apples are soft.
Pour into a bag and suspend over a bowl; let hang until juice no longer drips; do not squeeze bag.
Measure juice and bring it to a boil.
Add sugar gradually and cook rapidly until it begins to thicken.
When the last 2 drops on the spoon run together and "sheet off," remove jelly from stove.
Pour into hot jelly glasses and cover with paraffin.

Cranberry Conserves

1 pound cranberries   2 cups hot water
  (4 cups)   4 cups sugar
2 oranges   1 cup chopped nuts
1 cup chopped raisins

Grind raw cranberries and oranges through a food chopper.
Add hot water and bring to a boil.
Cook quickly until fruit is soft.
Add raisins, sugar and hot water.
Cook over moderate heat, stirring occasionally until thickened.
Remove from heat and add nuts.
Pour into hot jars and seal.

Peach Preserves

6 pounds peaches, sliced   ½ cup water
6 pounds sugar

Remove skins and seeds from peaches. Cut into thin
   slices.
Add water to sliced peaches and bring to a boil.
Add sugar.
When it has dissolved, cook rapidly until fruit is clear and
   syrup is thickened.
Pour into jars and seal.

Pear Marmalade

4 pounds sliced pears   3 oranges
4 pounds sugar

Remove peeling and core from pears.
Wash oranges and remove seeds.
Grind pears and oranges through food chopper.
Bring fruit to a boil and add sugar.
Cook until thick.
Pour into jars and seal.

Pineapple and Apricot Jam

1 pound dried apricots   1 cup sugar to each cup fruit
1 medium-sized fresh pine-
  apple

Soak apricots in water until soft.
Pare the pineapple and remove eyes.
Grind the drained apricots and pineapple. Measure.
Bring fruit to a boil and add sugar gradually (the same
   amount as fruit pulp).
Cook until fruit is clear and jam is thick.
Pour into jars and seal.

Quince Honey

2 cups grated quince   1 pint water
2 cups grated apples   4 pounds sugar

Wash and pare quinces and apples. Core and cut into quarters.
Grate or grind both fruits and mix together.
Add water to fruit and bring to a boil.
Add sugar gradually and stir until all has been dissolved.
Cook slowly until fruit is clear and mixture is thick (about 20 minutes).
Pour into jars and seal.

Red Raspberry Preserves

1 quart red raspberries   4 pounds sugar
2 cups tart apples   2 cups water

Wash and cap berries.
Cook sugar and water together until it spins a thread.
While it is cooking, pare and core apples.
Grind through food chopper.
Add ground apples to syrup and cook 4 minutes.
Then add the capped berries and cook 9 minutes longer.
Pour into hot jars and seal.

Strawberry Honey

2½ cups crushed strawberries   1⅛ cups water
3 pounds sugar   1 teaspoon powdered alum

Cook water and sugar together for 7 minutes.
Add crushed berries and boil for 5 minutes.
Add powdered alum and remove from heat.
Pour into jars and seal.

Candies
and
Confections

Chapter XV

Candy Crispies

1 cup sugar	½ package Rice Krispies (3½ oz.)
1 cup corn syrup	
1 cup thin cream	1 cup shredded coconut
½ package of corn flakes (4 oz.)	1 cup salted peanuts

Cook sugar, syrup and cream together until it forms a soft ball in cold water (236°).

Stir only until sugar is dissolved.

Crush corn flakes coarsely and mix with Krispies, coconut and peanuts.

Pour hot syrup over mixture and blend together.

Press into a flat, buttered pan.

Cut into squares when almost cold.

Chocolate Fudge

2 cups sugar	2 tablespoons butter
2 tablespoons corn syrup	1 teaspoon vanilla
¾ cup milk	1 cup chopped nuts
2 squares chocolate	

Cook sugar, syrup, milk and chocolate together until it forms a soft ball when dropped in cold water (236°).

Remove from heat and add butter.

Cool until you can hold your hand on the bottom of the pan (112°).

Add vanilla and nuts and beat until creamy.

Pour into buttered pan 4 x 8 inches.

Mark into squares and cool.

This is a creamy, moist and delicious fudge.

Caramel Candy

2 cups sugar	1 can evaporated milk (15 oz.)
2 cups syrup	
½ cup butter	1 teaspoon vanilla
⅛ teaspoon salt	1 cup chopped nuts

Bring sugar and syrup to a boil.
Add butter and salt.
When the boiling point has been reached again, add the milk slowly in a fine stream.
Keep bubbling, but do not cook rapidly.
Stir constantly to prevent scorching.
Cook syrup to 244° or until it makes a firm ball when dropped in cold water.
Remove from heat and add vanilla and chopped nuts.
Set in a pan of cold water to stop the cooking.
When slightly cooled, pour into a buttered pan 5 x 10 inches.
Mark with a heavy knife while slightly warm into 1 inch squares.
Let stand overnight and then wrap in waxed paper.
Care must be taken to prevent scorching while cooking.

Jiffy Chocolate Fudge (Uncooked)

15 oz. can condensed milk	⅛ teaspoon salt
2 (7 oz.) packages semisweet chocolate	1 teaspoon vanilla
	1 cup chopped nuts

Melt the chocolate in the top of double boiler. Add salt.
Add condensed milk and stir until well blended.
Remove from heat and add vanilla and nuts.
Pour into a flat, buttered pan 5 x 10 inches.
Chill for 2 to 3 hours. When firm, cut into squares.
Makes approximately 2 pounds.

Date Loaf Candy

3 cups sugar
1 cup milk
1 tablespoon butter
1½ cups chopped dates
1 cup walnuts or pecans, chopped
1 teaspoon vanilla

Cook sugar, milk and butter together until syrup forms a very soft ball when dropped in cold water (236°).
Add chopped dates and cook for 3 minutes longer.
Remove from heat and cool to lukewarm temperature.
Add nuts and vanilla. Beat until creamy.
Turn out on a damp cloth and roll.
Slice when cold.

Fondant

2 cups sugar
⅔ cup water
⅛ teaspoon salt
2 tablespoons white syrup
4 tablespoons marshmallow crème
1 teaspoon vanilla

Combine sugar, salt and water. Add syrup.
Stir only until sugar is dissolved.
Be careful not to get any sugar crystals from sides of the pan into syrup as it cooks.
Keep cover on pan part time so steam will keep crystals from forming.
Cook until syrup forms a soft ball when dropped in cold water (236°).
Pour on a greased platter and do not disturb until you can hold your hand on the bottom of the plate (112°).
Add vanilla and stir.
Place marshmallow crème in mixing bowl and pour cooled syrup over it.
Stir or knead until fondant becomes perfectly smooth.
Work into a ball, wrap in wax paper and allow to ripen in a tightly covered jar for at least 24 hours.

This may be used as filling for chocolate creams, or a base for nuts and fruits, or as mint patties.

Old-Fashioned Taffy

1 cup molasses
1 cup sugar
1 cup thin cream
2 tablespoons butter

1 teaspoon soda
1 cup finely chopped nuts
(optional)

Combine molasses, sugar and cream and bring to a boil.
Cook until it forms a firm ball when dropped in cold water (252° F).
Remove from heat and add butter and soda.
Add chopped nuts. Stir well.
Pour onto buttered plates and cool until it can be cut into small squares about ⅛ inch in diameter. This taffy is not pulled.

Peanut Brittle

2 cups sugar
1 cup white syrup
½ cup water
3 cups raw peanuts

1 teaspoon butter, melted
1 teaspoon soda
1 teaspoon vanilla

Combine sugar, syrup and water.
Cook to the soft-ball stage (236°).
Add peanuts and melted butter and continue cooking until syrup is a golden brown (290°). Stir during last few minutes of cooking.
Remove from heat and add soda and vanilla.
Stir until mixture thickens.
Pour into buttered tins and break into pieces when cold.
If roasted peanuts are used, add to syrup before removing from heat.

Coconut Candy

1½ cups brown sugar
3 cups granulated sugar
1⅓ cups milk
1 teaspoon butter

1 small coconut, grated or ground
1 teaspoon vanilla

Grind or grate the fresh coconut.
Mix sugar, milk and butter together.
Stir until sugar is dissolved.
When the mixture comes to a boil, add coconut.
Cook until a soft ball forms when dropped in cold water (236°).
Remove from heat and add vanilla.
Pour into a flat, buttered pan.
Cut into squares when cold.

Popcorn Balls

5 quarts popped corn
2 cups sugar
1½ cups water
½ cup white corn syrup

⅓ teaspoon salt
1 teaspoon vanilla
1 tablespoon vinegar

Pop the corn and remove the hard kernels.
Combine sugar, syrup and water. Bring to a boil, stirring only until sugar is dissolved.
Cook until it forms a hard ball when dropped in cold water (270°).
Add vinegar, salt and vanilla and blend into mixture.
Pour hot syrup slowly over the corn, stirring so that each kernel may be evenly coated.
Shape into balls and let stand in a cool place.
Each ball may be wrapped in wax paper if desired.
Peanuts may be added.

Index

The Author

Mary Emma Showalter comes from a long line
of good Mennonite cooks in the Shenandoah Val-
ley of Virginia. An intense interest in cooking has
led her to an intimate acquaintance with the best
in Mennonite cookery in America. Her work as a
dietitian has taken her to distant fields—a Yugo-
slav refugee camp in the Egyptian desert, the Lon-
don headquarters of Mennonite Central Commit-
tee, a children's home in northern England—but
she has never lost interest in traditional Mennonite
fare. The author was Professor of Home Economics at Eastern Mennonite College in Virginia
and head of the Home Economics Department. She
holds a doctor's degree from Pennsylvania State
University. Besides teaching she enjoys cooking in
her own kitchen and has had several articles on
foods published in national magazines.